F. W. Robinson MA

Brodie's Notes on Chaucer's

The Prologue to the Canterbury Tales

Pan Books London and Sydney

First published by James Brodie Ltd
New edition published 1976 by Pan Books Ltd
Cavaye Place, London SW10 9PG
This revised edition with parallel texts published 1980
    4 5 6 7 8 9
ISBN 0 330 50129 1
© James Brodie Ltd 1960
Filmset in Great Britain by
Northumberland Press Ltd, Gateshead, Tyne and Wear
Printed and bound by
Richard Clay (The Chaucer Press) Ltd, Bungay, Suffolk

Contents

To the student

A close reading of the *Tale* is the student's primary task.
These Notes will help to increase your understanding and
appreciation of the *Tale*, and to stimulate *your own* thinking
about it: *they are in no way intended as a substitute* for a thorough
knowledge of the work.

Editor's note and bibliography

Chaucer is our greatest comic poet, and *The Canterbury Tales* is his masterpiece. Yet Chaucer's poetry is not a subject for general reading, but of specialist study. The reason for this is that his language is not easy for the general reader to read and understand. The English language of the fourteenth century was different from the language we speak today, and some trouble must be taken in learning these differences before a proper understanding of the meaning can be gained. And further, when one has learned to read Chaucer and to understand the meaning, some knowledge is necessary of the age in which he lived, and his place in it, before the work of this colourful and humorous poet can be fully appreciated and enjoyed.

These notes are aimed primarily at students coming fresh to Chaucer in their studies of English literature. An attempt has been made to set out, as briefly and simply as possible, the areas of knowledge which are necessary for the proper understanding and appreciation of a selected text in the context of examination requirements at Ordinary and Advanced Levels. It is hoped, however, that the notes have been prepared in such a way that the student will enjoy the task of understanding and appreciating this wonderful poetry with its melodic style, gentle satire and rollicking humour, and even to acquire a taste for Chaucer which will lead to wider reading and a deeper appreciation of his work.

The Editor wishes to acknowledge his indebtedness to the various works he has studied, and particularly to the editions of Chaucer's works by Professors W. W. Skeat and F. N. Robinson (it is on the latter's work that the text of this edition is based – *The Complete Works of Geoffrey Chaucer*, 2nd ed., 1957, with revised punctuation and spelling by James Winny.

CUP, 1971); and the editions of several of Chaucer's *Tales* edited by F. W. Robinson and published by James Brodie Ltd.

Bibliography

For those who wish to carry their study of Chaucer beyond what is possible to include in a small volume of notes, a selection of books that may be helpful is listed below:

The Poet Chaucer, Nevill Coghill, OUP Paperbacks
An Introduction to Chaucer, Hussey, Spearing and Winny, CUP
English Social History, Trevelyan (Chaps 1 and 2) Longmans, also Penguin
Chaucer's World, ed. M. Hussey, CUP
Pelican Guide to English Literature, Vol. 1, The Age of Chaucer, Penguin

It is recommended that students should read a selection of the tales from the translation into modern verse by Nevill Coghill – *The Canterbury Tales*, translated by Nevill Coghill, Penguin Classics.

It is also recommended that students should listen to a recording of Chaucer read with the original pronunciation – *The Prologue to The Canterbury Tales*, read in Middle English by Nevill Coghill, Norman Davis and John Burrow, Argo Record Company, London, No. PLP 1001 (LP).

A brief description of
Chaucer's life and works

Geoffrey Chaucer was born about 1340 near the Tower of London. He was born into the age of Edward III, and of the Black Prince, into the Age of Chivalry and the magnificent court of Edward III with knights and ladies, heraldry and tournaments, minstrels and poetry, music and story-telling.

Chaucer entered into this rich and colourful courtly world at an early age, when he became a page in the household of the Countess of Ulster, wife to Lionel, later Duke of Clarence, and one of the sons of Edward III. This was clearly arranged by his parents, who had some contacts at Court. His mother's first husband had been Keeper of the King's Wardrobe, and there can be little doubt that she had something to do with the appointment of Chaucer's father as deputy to the King's Butler. The first record of Geoffrey Chaucer appears in an account book, dating from 1357, which records a payment by the royal household to a London tailor for a cloak, multi-coloured breeches and a pair of shoes for the young page Chaucer. It was in the Duke's great houses in London and Yorkshire that the young page would have learned the elegant and aristocratic code of manners, and made the acquaintance of the high and the noble. He would have learned French and Latin, the languages of the Court, the Church and the educated classes. It was also one of the duties of a page to play and sing, and to recite poetry.

The next record we have is that Chaucer was taken prisoner by the French in 1359, during one of the campaigns in The Hundred Years' War, and ransomed in the following year – the King himself contributing £16 (a very large sum in those days) of the money. So Chaucer must have seen active service in the French wars, probably as a squire attending on one of the nobles, like the squire in the *Canterbury Tales* who attended on the Knight, his father. For the upper classes, the experience of being a prisoner of war in the Age of Chivalry was not too uncomfortable. It was normal for the 'prisoner' to be entertained as a 'house guest' until the ransom was paid, and it is probable that during this enforced stay in France Chaucer became thoroughly versed in French literature, particularly the *Roman de la Rose* (the procedure manual, as it were, for 'courtly love'), which was to have such an important influence on his literary work.

After his ransom was paid, Chaucer returned to his Court duties, and soon in a more elevated position. He became one of the valets in attendance on the King. In 1366 his father died and his mother married again. It is probable that in the same year he married Philippa, daughter of Sir Payne Roet and sister of Katherine Swynford, the mistress and later third wife to John of Gaunt. Philippa was a lady-in-waiting to the Queen. As a valet to the King, Chaucer would carry candles 'before the King', tidy up his bedroom and attend to a variety of duties which were to become more and more concerned with affairs of state. In 1386 he was sent abroad on the official business of the Crown. About this time he was promoted from valet to palace official. It appears that Chaucer went soldiering again in 1369, probably on one of John of Gaunt's campaigns in Picardy. In 1370 he was abroad again on the King's service, and we can now see him becoming a trusted civil servant as he was frequently sent on missions to France, Flanders and Italy. During his visits to Italy on official business Chaucer took the opportunity to become familiar with Italian literature, most especially the works of Petrarch, Boccaccio and Dante, which were to influence much of his subsequent poetry.

In 1374 he was promoted to a senior position as Comptroller of Customs and Subsidy (for wool, skins and hides) at the Port of London, and the City of London bestowed on him the lease of a house in Aldgate.

From about 1380 Chaucer settled down to his life as senior customs official, as there is only one record of further journeys abroad. He must have been respected as a man of affairs, as he became a Justice of the Peace in 1385, and a Member of Parliament, or Knight of the Shire for Kent, soon afterwards.

It was during these years that Chaucer found time to write seriously. His early literary attempts were influenced considerably by French literature. Then, when John of Gaunt left the country in 1386 on an adventure to claim the crown of Castile, the King's uncle, the Duke of Gloucester, took charge of the country's affairs (Richard being not yet of age), and Chaucer suffered from the new influences in royal patronage. He lost his Comptrollership of Customs, he was not re-elected to Parliament and he had to give up his house in Aldgate. We even learn that he felt himself in danger of being sued for debt. Chaucer had now plenty of time to ponder and at this time he must have been preparing *The Canterbury Tales*.

In 1389 a rumour was abroad that the great Duke of Lancaster (Chaucer's patron John of Gaunt) was returning home. This helped the young King Richard II in taking over the reins of power from his uncle Gloucester. It has been stated that the young King Richard knew Chaucer and liked his poetry. There must be some substance in this, as shortly afterwards Chaucer was appointed Clerk of the King's Works. John of Gaunt returned to England in November 1389, and for the rest of his life Chaucer was to enjoy royal patronage and a comfortable living. It was in these years of semi-retirement that *The Canterbury Tales* were written. Alas, Chaucer died without having finished his masterpiece. His tomb in Westminster Abbey gives the date of his death – October 1400.

It seems probable that 1387 was the approximate date of commencement for *The Canterbury Tales*. Chaucer's renown rests mainly on this work, but in terms of volume the *Tales* form less than half of his writing which has come down to us.

Besides a number of shorter poems, there are five other major works in verse and two or three in prose. Chaucer's most important production during his first tentative years as a writer was his translation he probably made of the *Roman de la Rose*, the style and content of which was to have such a great influence on his writing. His first major poem was *The Book of the Duchess*, a poem steeped in the French tradition, written about 1370 to commemorate the death of Blanche, Duchess of Lancaster, and wife of his patron, John of Gaunt. This was the first of four love-vision poems, the others being *The House of Fame*, *The Parliament of Fowls* and *The Legend of Good Women* (whose date is doubtful). Chaucer's works can be conveniently grouped into three parts, the French period, the Italian period and the English period; and, generally speaking, the periods follow one another in chronological sequence. The French period showed influence of the *Roman de la Rose*, and included the love-vision poems. The Italian period (1380–5) is marked by the narrative poem *Troilus and Criseyde*, which rehandles a theme of the Italian poet Boccaccio. *Troilus and Criseyde* is a masterpiece, and is still considered to be the finest narrative poem in English, full of beauty and lyrical quality, and delightful humour in the character of Pandarus. The English period (1389–1400) is the last, and is the period when Chaucer reached his full maturity as a dramatic poet. This is the period of *The Canterbury Tales*, a collection of tales and tellers which is unique in English literature. Chaucer died before he could complete this great masterpiece.

It must be emphasized that these terms, 'French', 'Italian', 'English' for Chaucer's literary life only indicate predominant influences: the stories in *The Canterbury Tales* are drawn from far and wide; *The Knight's Tale*, for instance, again owes its theme to a story by Boccaccio.

The Pilgrims

The Knight

Chaucer's Knight had spent much of his life abroad, and was actually making the pilgrimage to Canterbury before going to his own home. His son had presumably met him somewhere between Harwich and London, with the yeoman who had brought the horses, possibly. The Knight had seen service in at least three spheres of fighting, for the places Chaucer mentions are some in the Eastern Mediterranean, some in the Western and the rest in the Baltic countries. He had also fought three times in the lists against infidels. Everywhere his reputation was of the highest, and he had not been spoilt by the distinctions he had won. In his demeanour he showed no aggressiveness; he was as meek as a maiden in word and manner. He made no display on the pilgrimage, but rode in a quiet-coloured tunic, soiled with his coat-of-mail. He loved knightly conduct, truth, honesty, generosity and courtly behaviour.

The Squire

His son, who had not yet won his spurs, was more showily dressed. His fashionably-cut grass-green jacket was dotted with white and red flowers; with his merry songs and music, he seemed to Chaucer as fresh as May itself. He was moderately tall, very active and very strong. In his raiding expeditions into the Low Countries he had conducted himself so as to stand high in the favour of his lady love. He had already acquired the arts which would appeal to her, for he could ride well, compose songs – both words and music – joust, dance, draw and write. Yet he was humble and ready to be of service. He was a worthy son of his distinguished father.

The Yeoman

A servant of the Knight, this Yeoman was skilled in forestry and the lore of hunting, and wore the bright green coat and hood associated with Robin Hood and his Merry Men. He carried also a long bow and a quiverful of peacock feathers. Some of his fellows were less skilled than he in preparing their arrows, for his arrows made the longest flights possible because of the perfectly-adjusted feathers. He had with him his horn, and a sword and buckler, while his wrist was guarded against the action of the bowstring. On his left side was an expensively mounted dagger. No wonder his face was brown, as he was always in the open air.

The Prioress

She was the Lady Superior of the Convent of St Leonards, near Stratford in Essex, or so the evidence seems to suggest. Madame Eglantine, for such Chaucer discovered her name to be, is described in such detail as to lead us to believe that Chaucer had some person in his mind and was not drawing a mere idealized picture as he had done for the first three characters. Perhaps the select audience to whom the poet doubtless read his tales would recognize the traits in her character and would be all the more amused at the portrait. She was daintiness itself in her behaviour at table, and though necessity compelled her to dip into the dish for her meat – for fingers were made before forks – she never dipped her fingers in deeply, for her whole aim was to imitate the manners of Court. She was a quaint mixture of the lady who had taken her vows and the lady who wished to stand well in the eyes of the great ones of the land. She could sing the service set out in the Missal, and speak French as it was taught in her school at Stratford. She carried her rosary as was proper, but it was of coral pink, with the larger beads of green, and a golden brooch hung from it. She smiled sweetly, and though she

swore by the saints as did all others in her days, she chose to
swear by one who was associated with daintiness in his handi-
work. Her womanly feelings were by no means smothered
under her black gown for she was tender to the little dogs she
kept as pets – though the Church law discouraged the
practice of keeping dogs at all – and fed them with the best
bread. Her headdress was not of the plainest, as would have
become one who had said farewell to vanities of the kind, but
it was neatly pleated; and though it should have covered
nearly all her forehead, Chaucer noted that her brow was at
least a span broad. Her cloak, moreover, was dainty. She had
her secretary with her and at least the one Priest who later
told the tale of Chantecleer and Partlet and the Fox, the
merriest and sweetest of all the stories told on the journey.

The Monk

Here follows a portrait of another ecclesiastic, the Monk, an
extremely handsome fellow. He was a *bon viveur*, delighting in
the fat swan which was forbidden to those who had taken
vows of poverty. His activities were, by their nature, not confined to the four walls of his monastery, for he had the over-
sight of the outlying lands and religious houses dependent
upon the mother-house itself. He thus found many an opportunity of enjoying his favourite sport of tracking the hare
with the help of his excellent horses and his hunting dogs. He
was as merry as the Squire was, though his merriment was of
another kind, and his dress was also gay, for Chaucer noticed
that his sleeves were trimmed with the most expensive fur,
and he wore a gold pin, carefully made. The poet seems to
have had some sympathy with his extra-mural activities: for
how can a monk serve the world if he shuts himself away from
it all day? Augustine was surely wrong in enjoining the
cloistered life. He was an excellent specimen of a churchman,
worthy to be an abbot, says the poet, and not a mere prior.

And yet when called upon for his tale, this worldly priest told about the downfall of men who had held illustrious positions, and so distressed his audience that the Knight had to beg him to tell something less doleful. There are no indications that Chaucer and his audience knew the particular monk who answered to the poet's description; he is a composite portrait suggesting that the ideals of many monks had sadly deteriorated, and pointing to the need for a reform in that part of the Church's activities.

The Friar

Chaucer now introduces a Franciscan Friar, who, carefree and jolly, was certainly out to make the best of both worlds while begging for alms for Holy Church. He was on the best of terms with the wealthy landowners and the well-to-do women of the district where he had permission to beg, for not only had he greater powers of granting absolution than the ordinary parish priest had, but his penances were lighter where he knew he himself would be treated to a good meal. After all, was not readiness to entertain a poor brother a sign that the sinner had repented? He could play the harp and was always a popular visitor when there was any festival of singing. He knew the inn-keepers and the barmaids better than the lepers and the beggar-women, for to be acquainted with these poor folk cannot in any way advance one in his profession. Yet he could beg for his community better than anyone else; so sweetly did he sing his gospel portion, and with such a pretty lisp, that even the very poorest women had to give him something before he went away. He dressed well with a double-worsted cape, and his strong body, his lily-white neck and his twinkling eyes made him look imposing. His name was Hubert.

The Merchant

He was engaged in the wool trade between England and Flanders, and was most anxious that the sea should be kept free from pirates between the ports of Ipswich and Middleburg. He was dressed smartly in a Flemish hat with neatly-fastened boots, and uttered his sentiments oracularly. He was busy also in lending money and in exchanging French coins for English, both of which transactions were against the law. If he knew his name, Chaucer was certainly wise in not revealing it.

The Clerk

Here is another of the churchmen, a candidate for Holy Orders and a student of philosophy. He spent all he could get from his friends in paying his fees to his university and in buying his books. He had no interest in gay clothes, or the fiddle, or the harp; nor did he see that his horse was properly fed or indeed that he himself was well nourished. His great concern was philosophy, and yet, as Chaucer slyly remarks, he had evidently not yet found the philosopher's stone, for he had but little gold in his treasure-chest. He was a pious man, however, and scorned to take a secular post while he was waiting for a benefice; and he prayed earnestly for the souls of those to whom he was indebted for the money wherewith to pay for his studies at Oxford.

The Sergeant of the Law

He was indeed a learned man, for he was one of that small group of lawyers who might be called to assist the king's judges in an emergency; he had studied all the judicial decisions which had been made since the law had been revolutionized by the Normans, and knew by heart all the

legal enactments. He specialized in buying up land, for
however complicated a title might seem to others, to him it
was simplicity itself; and no one could find any flaw in his
transactions. In spite of his large wardrobe of rich robes he
had chosen a striped gown for his journey, with simple orna-
mentations. Chaucer seems to have had in mind someone
known to his audience, for the details of this description are
particular rather than general.

The Franklin

He was the Sergeant's great friend and comrade. He was a
landed proprietor of gentle, if not noble, birth, and probably
also one whom Chaucer knew personally. His ruddy face was
surrounded with a white beard, and suggested one who was
fond of his food. Certainly he invited wayfarers to share his
good things, prepared by a cook who had to take care that all
he offered his master was just what he most relished. The
Franklin loved his early morning tit-bit of cake soaked in
wine, and prided himself on the excellent standard of his ale
and bread: it never varied. His cellar was full and his larder
held pies of fish and meat, while he himself took care to vary
his diet with the changing seasons of the year. He had often
been Member of Parliament for his county, had presided at
the sessions and had been sheriff too.

The Guildsmen

Perhaps Chaucer intended later to describe these five men
more fully, but he has put them all together as members of
a social or religious guild wearing the same livery. They were
wealthy men, as Chaucer could see from their silver-mounted
knives and money-pouches. Each of them seemed fit to
preside over the guild proceedings, and their wives would
surely not be averse to being called 'My Lady', and to having

their trains carried on feast nights as though they were princesses.

The Cook – Roger

These five rich men had possibly had unfortunate experience of how badly food can be cooked in a wayside tavern, for they had their own cook with them, who could prepare the favourite dishes of his masters. He knew a good glass of ale when he tasted one. It seemed to Chaucer a pity that he had an inflamed sore on his leg, but his skill as a cook could not be called in question.

The Shipman

As we might expect, he rode awkwardly on his hired hack. This master-mariner came from the far west of England, possibly from Dartmouth. He was a rascal, for while the merchant slept on shipboard the sailor had stolen many a draught of wine on the journey home from Bordeaux, for he had a very adaptable conscience. If he were attacked by pirates and gained the day he made the prisoners walk the plank. He was indeed a very skilful mariner, knowing all that was to be known about the seas between Sweden and the east coast of Spain. As Chaucer gives the name of his ship, and as there was at the time a ship of that name belonging to Dartmouth, we can assume that here again Chaucer had some individual in mind when he drew this sketch of the mariner.

The Doctor of Physic

He was an expert practitioner, for not only had he studied medicine and surgery, but he was well up in astrology which aided the mediæval doctor considerably. He knew in this way just the right moment for making the talismans which would help his patients to recover. He knew also the causes of all illnesses, and the best remedies. He had druggists who would supply him with what he wanted and who also sent him patients. He had read all the authorities on medicine, whether Greek, Arabic, or contemporary. He himself took great care to eat sparingly, and to save the big fees he received during the epidemics of plague. For after all, gold is a heart-tonic in medicine; and it is only right that the doctor should love gold especially.

The Wife of Bath – Alyson

It was certainly unfortunate that this excellent lady from near Bath was deaf. She was, however, an expert weaver who could excel the cloth-makers of Ypres and Ghent in the Low Countries. Her importance was such that she would allow no one to take precedence of her at the offertory. She wore on her head on Sundays coverings that must have weighed ten pounds. They were of the finest texture: her stockings were of bright red, and her shoes supple and new. Her countenance was ruddy, and attractive, though her teeth were too wide apart. She had had five husbands, but the poet reserved his comments on this point till later. She rode comfortably astride her horse, for she had had great experience in travelling, for she had three times been as far as Jerusalem as a pilgrim. She had also visited the shrines at Rome, Bologna, and Cologne as well as the Holy Place at Santiago in Galicia. Her neck-covering was of the best, and she wore a very large hat. She could always find something to say to the company. She knew all the devices of lovemaking, and was an expert on this subject too.

The Poor Parson

He was of lowly origin, and his brother was a worker on the land; but though he was poor he was rich in holy thought and deed. He set himself to preach the Gospel of Christ, which he himself followed. The law bade him to excommunicate those who did not pay their tithes; but so reluctant was he to take this extreme step that he would rather pay the sum out of his own savings, poor though he himself was. He was conscientious in visiting his people, though his parish was so scattered, and nothing would keep him from his duty. He taught that a priest should set a good example to his flock; for if the priest grows corrupt, what wonder is it if an ignorant man does so too? Other priests forsook their parishes and took lucrative posts under the Church's ægis in London; he, like the Good Shepherd of the Gospels, stayed with the sheep lest the wolf should do them harm. His aim was to draw people to Heaven by good example; but if he found an obstinate sinner, he was quite capable of reproving him sharply on occasion. He wanted no outward signs of deference. He taught the teaching of Christ, and followed it himself first of all.

The Plowman

The parish priest's brother was a small farmer, not a ploughman in our modern sense. But he did the most menial tasks on the farm, and would toil for a sick neighbour or one in distress without any thought of reward. He paid his tithes regularly, and loved God first, and then his neighbour as himself. He was dressed in a smock, and rode on a mare, an indifferent kind of mount.

The Miller

A burly fellow like this would be useful on a journey on which there was always the risk of being attacked by robbers. Wherever he went he took the prize for wrestling, and was so strong that he could lift any door from its hinges or even break it by running at it with his head. The hair on his face was as brown as a fox's, and on the very tip of his nose grew a wart with a red hairy tuft. His nostrils were wide and black, and his mouth was as wide as a furnace. He was a loud talker and a foul-mouthed buffoon, and had a store of scurrilous tales. He ground the corn for the villagers, but managed to take three times the right dues for the service. He wore a white miller's coat and a blue hood, and led the procession from the Tabard, blowing on his bagpipes.

The Manciple

He was an under-servant in one of the Inns of Court, and his duty was to buy in food for the thirty masters whose servant he was. He was an expert at this work, for he took care to be at the market before his rivals, and so came off best. Surely, says Chaucer, it is a good gift of God that a man of so little education should be so efficient a servant of so many learned men. There were at least a dozen lawyers in that house who could take over the whole management of the estate of any lord in the land, and yet in his own line this fellow excelled them all.

The Reeve – Oswald

He was a near neighbour of the Miller, as the poet tells us later, but they were not on speaking terms. The Miller headed the procession of pilgrims, but the Reeve was at the back. Chaucer must have known this steward, for he gives details of his house and his village, and it was a village with which Chaucer himself had had some connection. His figure may have been odd, but he was good at his work. No one could get the better of him, or prove him a defaulter, and all the other servants were as afraid of him as of the plague; yet he was engaged in underhand practices, for he had some of his lord's money which he pretended was his own, and this he would lend his master, and receive for the loan a considerable gift in kind. However, he was a good steward, though he had been brought up as a carpenter. He rode a good horse, and wore a long outer coat of blue-gray. He also carried a rusty sword. His house at Baldeswell in Norfolk was well placed on a heath.

The Summoner

He was an officer in the archdeacon's court, and his duty was to summon offenders against ecclesiastical law to appear before the tribunal. No wonder children were afraid of his face, which perhaps showed many of the distinguishing signs of leprosy. His tastes were crude, and his morals cruder still. He winked at immoral conduct among his friends, and taught them not to be afraid of excommunication, for a money payment would put everything right again. Chaucer had to insert a protest against his disregard of the extreme penalty of the Church. He was quite an unintelligent fellow, who repeated Latin tags from documents when he was drunk on the strong ale he delighted in. Yet this was the fellow who had under his thumb all the young people of the neighbourhood, and was their adviser in all things. As a piece of foolery he had on his head a kind of bush such as was used to attract attention to an ale house by the road-side; and he carried for a shield a kind of trencher made of bread.

The Pardoner

He was attached to the cell at Charing Cross, whose mother-house was at Roncesvalles, in Navarre, where the Paladins of Charlemagne had fought. He was the Summoner's friend, and they were two of a kind. He had come from Rome direct to London with a wallet stuffed full of pardons, 'all hot' and ready for sale. Thin though his voice was, he sang with his full power the very unecclesiastical ditty of 'Come hither, love, to me', his comrade, the Summoner, singing the accompaniment in so deep a drone that never a trumpet had so base a sound. His long yellow hair hung over his shoulders, for he wore no hood on this holiday. Yet he was well skilled in his craft. He had relics which would draw pence or farthings from the ignorant clergy who believed his tales, and thus made dupes of those he visited. Yet he was a fine preacher; he read the lesson well, but his speciality was singing the offertory to win silver for the church.

The Host – Harry Bailley

He was fit, from his manly appearance, to have been a major-domo in one of the guild halls, for even in Cheapside there could be found no finer specimen of a man. Outspoken as he was, he was well bred and excellent at amusing his guests. He made the proposal that the travellers should tell tales for a prize as they rode to Canterbury, and he was shrewd enough to stipulate that the dinner to the winner should be eaten at his own Tabard Inn in Southwark. He called all his guests early in the morning, and after they had ridden about two miles along the Old Kent Road he halted the procession in order to find by lot who was to tell the first tale. When the Clerk seemed in a brown study he rallied him till he stood ready to choose one of the straws; he spoke with great politeness to the Lady Prioress, and bade the Knight make the first choice from the straws in the heap in his hand. By luck the lot fell to the Knight, who forthwith told the first story.

The Prologue to *The Canterbury Tales*

Here bygynneth the Book of the Tales of Caunterbury.

  Whan that Aprille with his shoures soote
The droghte of March hath perced to the roote,
And bathed every veyne in swich licóur,
Of which vertú engendred is the flour;
Whan Zephirus eek with his swete breeth   5
Inspired hath in every holt and heeth
The tendre croppes, and the yonge sonne
Hath in the Ram his halfe cours y-ronne,
And smale fowles maken melodye
That slepen al the night with open ye,—   10
 So priketh hem nature in hir coráges,—
Thanne longen folk to goon on pilgrimages,
And palmeres for to seken straunge strondes,
To ferne halwes, couthe in sondry londes;
And specially, from every shires ende   15
Of Engelond, to Caunterbury they wende,
The hooly blisful martir for to seke,
That hem hath helpen whan that they were seeke.

  Bifel that in that seson on a day,
In Southwerk at the Tabard as I lay,   20
Redy to wenden on my pilgrimage
To Caunterbury with ful devout corage,
At night were come into that hostelrye.
Wel nyne-and-twenty in a companye,
Of sondry folk, by aventure y-falle   25
In felawshipe, and pilgrims were they alle,
That toward Caunterbury wolden ryde.

The chambres and the stables weren wyde,
And wel we weren esed atte beste.
And shortly, whan the sonne was to reste,   30
So hadde I spoken with hem everichon,
That I was of hir felawshipe anon,
And made foreward erly for to ryse,
To take oure wey, ther as I yow devyse.

The Prologue to *The Canterbury Tales*

Here begins the book of the Canterbury Tales.

When the month of April with its sweet showers has pierced the drought of March to the root of every plant and bathed every vein in that liquid through whose power the flower is produced, when Zephyr (i.e. the West Wind) also with his sweet breath has given life to the tender shoots in every copse and on every heath, when the young sun has completed his half-course in the Ram and small birds that sleep the whole night long with their eyes open sing, because Nature gives their hearts the urge, this is the time that people long to go on pilgrimages, and pilgrims are eager to seek strange shores and visit the distant shrines that are famous in various lands; and even from the farthest limits of every shire in England they journey to Canterbury to seek the holy blessed martyr who helped them when they lay sick.

It chanced that one day during that time of the year, as I was spending the night at the Tabard in Southwark, intending to proceed with a very devout mind on my pilgrimage to Canterbury, a company of some twenty-nine people of all sorts and types arrived towards nightfall at the inn. These had fallen into friendship by mere chance and they were all pilgrims who intended to ride to Canterbury.

The rooms and stables of the inn were spacious and we were accommodated in the very best style; and, to be brief, when the sun had set, I had chatted with everyone of them and straightway became part of their company and we agreed to rise early in order to make our way to the place I have already mentioned to you.

But nathelees, whil I have tyme and space,   35
Er that I ferther in this tale pace,
Me thinketh it accordant to resoun
To telle yow al the condicioun
Of ech of hem, so as it semed me,
And whiche they were and of what degree,   40
And eek in what array that they were inne;
And at a Knight than wol I first bigynne.

  A Knight ther was and that a worthy man,
That fro the tyme that he first bigan
To riden out, he loved chivalrye,   45
Trouthe and honour, fredom and curtesye.
Ful worthy was he in his lordes werre,
And therto hadde he riden, no man ferre,
As wel in Cristendom as in hethenesse,
And ever honoured for his worthinesse.   50
  At Alisaundre he was whan it was wonne;
Ful ofte tyme he hadde the bord bigonne
Aboven alle nacions in Pruce.
In Lettow hadde he reysed and in Ruce,—
No Cristen man so ofte of his degree.   55
In Gernade at the seege eek hadde he be
Of Algezir, and riden in Belmarye.
At Lyeys was he, and at Satalye,
Whan they were wonne; and in the Grete See
At many a noble armee hadde he be.   60

  At mortal batailles hadde he been fiftene,
And foughten for oure feith at Tramyssene
In listes thryes, and ay slayn his foo.
This ilke worthy knight hadde been also
Somtyme with the lord of Palatye   65
Agayn another hethen in Turkye;
And evermore he hadde a sovereyn prys.
And though that he were worthy, he was wys,
And of his port as meeke as is a mayde.
He never yet no vileynye ne sayde   70
In al his lyf unto no maner wight.
He was a verray, parfit, gentil knight.

But even so, while I have the time and opportunity before I go any farther with this story, I think it reasonable to tell you the complete social standing of each of them, just as it appeared to me, what sort of men they were, of what degree and in what clothes they were dressed. I shall begin, then, with a Knight.

There was a Knight, an honourable man, who, from the time that he first became a soldier, loved knightly conduct, truth, honour, freedom and courteous manners. He had been brave and capable in his Lord's war and, moreover, no man had served farther afield, not only in Christendom but also in heathen countries, and he had always been held in the highest respect for his moral excellence. He was at Alexandria when it was captured and very often in Prussia he had occupied the most honoured place at table above all ranks. He had served as a soldier in Lithuania and Russia. Indeed, no Christian man of equal rank had served as often as he. He had also been in Granada at the time of the siege of Algeciras and had served in Ben-Marin. He was at Ayas and Attalia when they were captured and had accompanied many magnificent expeditions to the Mediterranean Sea.

He had been present at fifteen fierce battles, had fought in three tournaments for our faith at Tlemsen and had killed his adversary every time. This renowned Knight had also been once with the lord of Palatia, still another heathen ruler of Turkey. He always gained very great renown *but*, although he was brave, he was prudent and as meek as a girl in his behaviour. He had never uttered foul language in his whole life to any person whatsoever. He was a true, perfect and refined Knight.

But for to tellen yow of his array,
His hors were goode, but he was nat gay;
Of fustian he wered a gypoun   75
Al bismotered with his habergeoun;
For he was late y-come from his viáge,
And wente for to doon his pilgrimage.

With him ther was his sone, a yong Squyér,
A lovyere and a lusty bacheler,   80
With lokkes crulle, as they were leyd in presse.
Of twenty yeer of age he was, I gesse.
Of his stature he was of evene lengthe,
And wonderly delyvere and of greet strengthe;
And he hadde been somtyme in chivachye,   85
In Flaundres, in Artoys and Picardye,
And born him wel, as of so litel space,
In hope to stonden in his lady grace.

Embrouded was he, as it were a meede
Al ful of fresshe floures whyte and reede;   90
Singynge he was or floytynge al the day;
He was as fressh as is the month of May.
Short was his gowne, with sleves longe and wyde;
Wel coude he sitte on hors, and faire ryde;
He coude songes make and wel endite,   95
Juste and eek daunce and wel purtreye and write.
So hoote he lovede that by nightertale
He sleep no more than dooth a nightyngale.
Curteys he was, lowly and servysable,
And carf biforn his fader at the table.   100

A Yeman hadde he and servantz no moo
At that tyme, for him liste ryde soo;
And he was clad in cote and hood of grene;
A sheef of pecok arwes bright and kene
Under his belt he bar ful thriftily—   105
Wel coude he dresse his takel yemanly—
His arwes drouped noght, with fetheres lowe—
And in his hand he bar a mighty bowe.
A not-heed hadde he with a broun visage.

But, to tell you about his clothes, although he had a good horse, he himself was not finely dressed. He wore a fustian tunic, soiled all over by his coat of mail, for he had only lately returned from his travels and had decided to fulfil his pilgrimage straightaway.

With him was his son, a young Squire, a lover and a jolly probationer, whose locks of hair were curled just as if he kept them in a press. I suppose he was about twenty years of age. In physique, he was moderately tall, amazingly agile and of great strength. He had at one time taken part in raids in Flanders, Artois and Picardy and, considering the short time he had served, had conducted himself excellently in the hope of gaining his lady's favour.

His short gown was embroidered like a meadow covered with fresh flowers, both white and red. He sang or fluted the whole day long and was as fresh as the month of May. He wore a short gown with long, wide sleeves. As well as being able to sit a horse and ride admirably, he could compose songs, both the words and music, joust in tournaments, dance, draw and write well; and he was so passionate in love that he slept no more at nightfall than a nightingale. He was courteous, humble and practical and carved at table in his father's presence.

With him at that time was a Yeoman but no other servant, for it was his pleasure to ride in that manner. The Yeoman was dressed in a coat and hood of green, carrying very carefully under his belt a sheaf of bright, sharp arrows fitted with peacock feathers. He took care of his equipment in the true manner of a yeoman, his arrows never falling short because of weak feathers. In his hand he carried a long-bow and he had a closely-cropped head and a brown face.

Of woodecraft wel coude he al the usage. 110
Upon his arm he bar a gay bracer,
And by his syde a swerd and a bokeler,
And on that oother syde a gay daggere
Harneysed wel and sharpe as point of spere;
A Cristofre on his brest of silver shene; 115
An horn he bar, the bawdrik was of grene.
A forster was he soothly, as I gesse.

   Ther was also a nonne, a Prioresse,
That of hir smylyng was ful simple and coy;
Hir gretteste ooth was but by seint Loy, 120
And she was cleped madame Eglentyne.
Ful wel she song the service divyne,
Entuned in hir nose ful semely;
And Frenssh she spak ful faire and fetisly
After the scole of Stratford-atte-Bowe, 125
For Frenssh of Paris was to hire unknowe.
At mete wel y-taught was she with-alle,
She leet no morsel from hir lippes falle,
Ne wette hir fingres in hir sauce depe;
Wel coude she carie a morsel, and wel kepe 130
That no drope ne fille upon hir brest.
In curtesye was set ful muchel hir lest.
Hire over-lippe wyped she so clene,
That in her coppe ther was no ferthing sene
Of grece, whan she dronken hadde hir draughte. 135
Ful semely after hir mete she raughte,
And sikerly she was of greet disport,
And ful plesaunt and amyable of port,
And peyned hire to countrefete chere
Of court, and been estatlich of manere, 140
And to ben holden digne of reverence.

   But for to speken of hir conscience,
She was so charitable and so pitous
She wolde wepe if that she saugh a mous
Caught in a trappe, if it were deed or bledde. 145
Of smale houndes hadde she, that she fedde
With rosted flessh, or milk and wastel breed;
But soore weep she, if oon of hem were deed,
Or if men smoot it with a yerde smerte;
And al was conscience and tendre herte. 150

Knowing all the tricks of hunting, he bore a fine guard upon his arm, a sword and buckler on one side and a beautiful, well-decorated dagger, that was as sharp as the point of a spear, on the other side. On his breast he wore an image of St Christopher made of shining silver. He also carried a horn and wore a green baldric. I feel sure he was a true forester.

We also had in our company a Nun, a Prioress, whose smile was modest and demure. She was called Madam Eglantine and the severest oath she uttered was only by St Loy. She sang the Divine Service very sweetly, intoning it politely through her nose. Although she did not have a Parisian accent, she spoke French competently and gracefully in the fashion of the school of Stratford le Bow.

At mealtimes, moreover, she was well-bred, allowing no morsel to fall from her lips nor dipping her fingers too deeply in the saucer. Indeed, she managed a morsel of food so well that no crumb fell upon her breast. She took the greatest delight in cultivating charming manners. Not only did she wipe her upper lip so clean that no trace of grease was visible in her cup when she had taken a drink but she also reached for her food in the politest manner. She was certainly very cheerful and had a pleasant and friendly disposition. She went to great trouble to imitate courtly behaviour, to possess an imposing manner and to be held in high respect.

As far as her nature was concerned, she was so loving and compassionate that she would weep if she saw a mouse caught in a trap if it were dead or bleeding. She kept some small dogs that she fed with roast meat or milk and cake-bread, while she wept grievously if one of them died or if anyone struck one of them sharply with a stick. She was the embodiment of consideration and tender-heartedness.

Ful semely hir wympel pinched was;
Hir nose tretys, hir eyen greye as glas,
Hir mouth ful smal and ther-to softe and reed,
But sikerly she hadde a fair forheed;
It was almoost a spanne brood I trowe,   155
For, hardily, she was nat undergrowe.
Ful fetis was hir cloke, as I was war;
Of smal coral aboute hir arm she bar
A peire of bedes gauded al with grene,
And ther-on heng a brooch of gold ful shene,   160
On which ther was first write a crowned A,
And after, *Amor vincit omnia.*
  Another nonne with hire hadde she,
That was hir chapeleyne, and preestes thre.

  A Monk ther was, a fair for the maistrye,   165
An outrydere that lovede venerye,
A manly man, to been an abbot able.
Ful many a deyntee hors hadde he in stable,
And whan he rood men mighte his brydel heere
Gynglen in a whistlynge wynd als cleere,   170
And eek as loude, as dooth the chapel-belle,
Ther as this lord was kepere of the celle.
  The reule of seint Maure or of seint Beneit,
By-cause that it was old and som-del streit,—
This ilke Monk leet olde thinges pace   175
And heeld after the newe world the space.
He yaf nat of that text a pulled hen
That seith that hunters beth nat hooly men,
Ne that a monk whan he is recchelees
Is likned til a fissh that is waterlees;   180
This is to seyn, a monk out of his cloystre.

But thilke text heeld he nat worth an oystre;
And I seyde his opinioun was good.
What sholde he studie and make him-selven wood,
Upon a book in cloystre alwey to poure,   185
Or swynken with his handes and laboure
As Austin bit? how shal the world be served?
Lat Austin have his swynk to him reserved.
Therefore he was a prikasour aright;
Grehoundes he hadde, as swift as fowel in flight: 190
Of prikyng and of huntyng for the hare
Was al his lust, for no cost wolde he spare.

Her kerchief was pleated very neatly, her nose was well-proportioned, her eyes as grey as glass and her mouth was small, soft and red. She had an attractive forehead, a span broad, I should say, and she herself was certainly of a goodly height. Her cloak, I noticed, was very neat, and over her arm she carried a pair of small coral beads with paternosters of green stone. Hanging from them was a brooch of very bright gold on which was written an encrowned 'A' followed by 'Amor Vincit Omnia'.

Another Nun, who acted as her Secretary, was with her as well as three Priests.

In the company was an exceedingly fine type of Monk, an out-rider who loved hunting. He was a fine figure of a man, fit, I should think, to be an Abbot. He kept many excellent horses in his stables and, when he went riding, his bridle could be heard jingling in the whistling wind as clear and as loud as the bell of the Chapel where he was Prior of the monastic house. Because the rules of St Maurus or St Beneit were old and somewhat strict, this Monk disregarded old customs and followed the current fashion. He did not care 'a plucked hen' (i.e. he did not care twopence) for that text which says that hunters are not devout men or that a monk, who is negligent in his duties, is like a fish out of water (I mean by that, a monk outside his cloister).

He did not think that individual text was worth an oyster and I agreed with him that his opinions were sound. Why should he study and make himself mad through poring over a book in his cloister all the time or toiling and labouring with his hands, as St Augustine bids? How can one perform service to the world in that way? Let St Augustine keep his work to himself. But he could certainly be called a hard rider because he owned greyhounds that could run as swiftly as birds in flight, and his whole delight was centred on tracking and hunting the hare, a pleasure on which he spared no expense.

I seigh his sleves ypurfiled at the hond
With grys, and that the fyneste of a lond;
And for to festne his hood under his chin   195
He hadde of gold y-wroght a curious pin;
A love-knotte in the gretter ende ther was.
His heed was balled, that shoon as any glas,
And eek his face as it hadde been anoynt.
He was a lord ful fat and in good poynt;   200
Hise eyen stepe and rollynge in his heed,
That stemed as a forneys of a leed;
His bootes souple, his hors in greet estaat.
Now certeinly he was a fair prelaat.
He was nat pale, as a forpyned goost: 205
A fat swan loved he best of any roost;
His palfrey was as broun as is a berye.

   A Frere ther was, a wantown and a merye,
A limitour, a ful solempne man.
In alle the ordres foure is noon that can   210
So muchel of daliaunce and fair langage;
He hadde maad ful many a mariage
Of younge wommen at his owne cost.
   Unto his ordre he was a noble post;
And wel biloved and famulier was he   215
With frankeleyns over-al in his contree;
And with worthy wommen of the toun,
For he hadde power of confessioun,
As seyde him-self, moore than a curat,
For of his ordre he was licenciat.   220

Ful swetely herde he confessioun,
And plesaunt was his absolucioun.
He was an esy man to yeve penaunce
Ther as he wiste to have a good pitaunce;
For unto a povre ordre for to yive   225
Is signe that a man is wel y-shrive;
For, if he yaf, he dorste make avaunt
He wiste that a man was repentaunt:
For many a man so hard is of his herte
He may nat wepe althogh hym soore smerte;   230
Therfore in stede of wepynge and preyeres
Men mote yeve silver to the povre freres.

I noticed that his sleeves were trimmed at the wrist with the finest grey fur in the country. Fastening his hood under his chin was an elaborate skilfully-wrought golden pin which had a love-knot at its larger end. Both his bald head and his face, just as if he had been anointed, shone like a piece of glass but, although his figure was very stout, he was in the best of condition. His sparkling eyes shone like a furnace and goggled about. He wore supple boots and rode on a horse that was in fine condition. Without any shadow of doubt he was an excellent specimen of a Churchman. He was not pale like a tormented spirit. Indeed, he loved a fat swan best of any roast. As for his horse, that was as brown as a berry.

There was with us as well a Limiter, a pleasant but pompous wanton. No one in the four monastic orders had so much small talk and easy conversation. He had officiated at the marriages of many young women without a fee.

He was also an excellent pillar of his own monastic order and was popular and on friendly terms everywhere in his own district with wealthy landowners and the well-to-do women of the town, for he had, as he said himself, more extensive faculties for Confession than a parish priest because he was a licentiate in his order.

He heard Confession most indulgently while his Absolution, too, was most pleasant. He gave an easy penance whenever he was certain of receiving a liberal gift of food; for it was sure proof that a person was truly absolved if he gave unto a member of a poor monastic order. If a person gave something, the friar could well boast that he knew that the individual was repentant. And so, instead of weeping and praying, one ought to give silver to the poor friars, because many men are so hard of heart that they cannot weep even though they feel it very deeply.

His tipet was ay farsed ful of knyves
And pinnes, for to yeven yonge wyves;
And certeinly he hadde a murye note;   235
Wel coude he singe and pleyen on a rote:
Of yeddynges he bar outrely the prys;
His nekke whit was as the flour-de-lys;
Ther-to he strong was as a champioun.

He knew the tavernes wel in al the toun   240
And everich hostiler and tappestrere
Bet than a lazar or a beggestere;
For unto swich a worthy man as he
Acorded nat, as by his facultee,
To have with sike lazars aqueyntaunce;   245
It is nat honest, it may nat avaunce,
Fór to deelen with no swich poraille,
But al with riche and selleres of vitaille.
But over-al, ther as profit sholde aryse,
Curteys he was and lowly of servyse;   250
Ther nas no man nowher so vertuous.

He was the beste beggere in his hous,
For thogh a widwe hadde noght a sho,
So pleasaunt was his *In principio*,
Yet wolde he have a ferthing er he wente: 255
His purchas was wel bettre than his rente.
And rage he coude, as it were right a whelpe.
  In love-dayes ther coude he muchel helpe,
For there he was not lyk a cloysterer
With a thrédbare cope, as is a povre scolér,   260
But he was lyk a maister, or a pope;
Of double worstede was his semycope,
That rounded as a belle out of the presse.
Somwhat he lipsed for his wantownesse,
To make his Englissh swete upon his tonge,   265
And in his harpyng, whan that he hadde songe,
Hise eyen twynkled in his heed aright
As doon the sterres in the frosty night.
  This worthy limitour was cleped Huberd.

  A Marchant was ther with a forked berd,   270
In motteleye, and hye on horse he sat;
Upon his heed a Flaundrissh bever hat;
His bootes clasped faire and fetisly;

His short cape was always stuffed full of knives and pins as presents for beautiful women; and he certainly had a cheerful manner. He was skilled in singing and playing on a harp and won the prize outright for his ballads. His neck was as white as the fleur-de-lis and he was as strong as a prize-fighter as well.

He was well acquainted with the taverns in every town and was on more familiar terms with every innkeeper and barmaid than with lepers or beggarwomen, for it was not sensible that such an excellent man as he, considering his profession, should make the acquaintance of sick lepers. He thought it was neither honourable nor profitable to be friendly with such poor folk, but, in his opinion, it was best to have dealings only with the rich and sellers of provisions. Wherever, therefore, he could reap profit, he was courteous and humble in the performance of his duty and, under these circumstances, no other person showed such virtue.

He was the best beggar in his friary, for though a widow did not own a shoe, yet his 'In Principio' was so sweet that he would beg a farthing before he left her. The gains from his begging were much more lucrative than his regular income. He could also romp like a puppy.

At peace-making conferences he rendered great help, for on these occasions he was more like a master or a Pope than a poor scholar with a threadbare cope who lives in a cloister. His short cape, made of double worsted, was rounded like a bell just out of a press. By way of affectation he lisped now and then in order to make his English speech sound attractive and, when he sang to the accompaniment of his harp, his eyes twinkled in his head like stars on a frosty night.

Hubert was the name of this respected Limiter.

A Merchant with a forked beard was there too. He was dressed in motley clothes and sat high on his horse. He wore a Flemish beaver hat on his head and his boots were neatly fastened.

His resons he spak ful solempnely,
Sounynge alway thencrees of his winnyng.   275
He wolde the see were kept for any thing
Bitwixe Middelburgh and Orewelle.
Wel coude he in eschaunge sheeldes selle.
This worthy man ful wel his wit bisette;
Ther wiste no wight that he was in dette,   280
So estatly was he of his governaunce
With his bargaynes and with his chevisaunce.
For sothe he was a worthy man with-alle;
But, sooth to seyn, I noot how men him calle.

A Clerk ther was of Oxenford also   285
That unto logik hadde longe y-go.
As leene was his hors as is a rake,
And he nas nat right fat, I undertake,
But looked holwe and ther-to sobrely;
Ful thredbare was his overest courtepy;   290
For he hadde geten him yet no benefice,
Ne was so worldly for to have office;
For hym was lever have at his beddes heed
Twenty bookes clad in blak or reed
Of Aristotle and his philosophye,   295
Than robes riche, or fithele, or gay sautrye.
But al be that he was a philosophre,
Yet hadde he but litel gold in cofre;
But al that he mighte of his freendes hente
On bookes and on lernynge he it spente,   300
And bisily gan for the soules preye
Of hem that yaf him wher-with to scoleye.
Of studie took he moost cure and moost heede
Noght o word spak he moore than was neede,
And that was seyd in forme and reverence,   305
And short and quik and ful of hy sentence.
Sounynge in moral vertu was his speche,
And gladly wolde he lerne and gladly teche.

A Sergeant of the Lawe, war and wys,
That often hadde been at the Parvys,   310
Ther was also, ful riche of excellence.
Discreet he was and of greet reverence;
He semed swich, hise wordes weren so wise.

He proclaimed his opinions very pompously and was for ever boasting about the way his profits were increasing. He wished that the sea between Middelburgh and Orwell should be kept free of pirates at all costs. He knew all about the exchange of French crowns. This fine fellow used his intelligence so skilfully and managed his bargains and money-lending in such a ceremonious and lofty manner that no one guessed he was in debt. To tell you the truth, I did not know his name but on the whole he was a worthy fellow.

Another pilgrim with us was a Clerk of Oxford, who had for a long time devoted himself to the study of logic. His horse was as thin as a rake and he himself, I assure you, was by no means fat. As well as being solemn he looked half-starved. His outer short-cloak was threadbare, for he had not as yet secured a Church appointment for himself. He was not worldly-minded enough to accept a secular appointment and preferred to have twenty books about Aristotle's philosophy, bound in black or red, at his bed-side than fine cloth robes or a fiddle or a beautiful psaltery. Although he was a philosopher, he had very little gold in his strong-box because all that he could get from his friends he spent on books and knowledge and prayed earnestly for the souls of those who gave him the wherewithal to be a scholar. Study was his dearest care and interest. Not one word more than was necessary did he speak and everything was delivered with propriety and modesty, briefly and quickly, with deep meaning. His speech was full of moral sentiments; and he both learnt himself and taught others most gladly.

Another pilgrim among us was a Sergeant of the Law, who was alert and prudent, full of sterling qualities and who had taken part many times in conferences in the Inns of Court. As his speech was so wise and discreet, he seemed to be held in deep respect.

Justice he was ful often in assise,
By patente and by pleyn commissioun,   315
For his science and for his heigh renoun.
Of fees and robes hadde he many oon.
So greet a purchasour was nowher noon;
Al was fee simple to him in effect;
His purchasyng mighte nat been infect.   320
Nowher so bisy a man as he ther nas,
And yet he semed bisier than he was.
  In termes hadde he caas and doomes alle
That from the tyme of king William were falle;
Ther-to he coude endite and make a thing,   325
Ther coude no wight pinche at his writyng;
And every statut coude he pleyn by rote.
He rood but hoomly in a medlee cote,
Girt with a ceint of silk with barres smale;
Of his array telle I no lenger tale.   330

  A Frankeleyn was in his companye;
Whit was his berd as is the dayesye;
Of his complexioun he was sangwyn.
Wel loved he by the morwe a sop in wyn;
To liven in delyt was ever his wone,   335
For he was Epicurus owne sone,
That heeld opinion that pleyn delyt
Was verraily felicitee parfyt.
An householdere, and that a greet, was he;
Seint Julian he was in his contree;   340
His breed, his ale, was alweys after oon;
A bettre envyned man was nowher noon.

Withoute bakemete was never his house,
Of fissh and flessh, and that so plentevous
It snewed in his hous of mete and drinke,   345
Of alle deyntees that men coude thinke.
After the sondry sesons of the yeer,
So chaunged he his mete and his soper.
Ful many a fat partrich hadde he in mewe,
And many a breem and many a luce in stewe.   350
Wo was his cook but-if his sauce were
Poynaunt and sharp, and redy al his gere.
His table dormant in his halle alway
Stood redy covered al the longe day.

He had on several occasions acted as a judge in the County Court, holding both letters of appointment he had received from the King and full powers vested in him by the Commission, and had gained a large number of fees and robes through his learned writings and his high reputation. There was nowhere else such a great buyer of land and, in fact, he gave us the impression that land-transactions were so simple that everything could be regarded as absolute property. His conveyancing could never be declared to have no legal force. Nowhere was there such a busy man as he and yet he pretended that he was busier than he really was.

In addition to knowing all the cases and judicial decisions that had occurred since the time of King William in precise terms he could frame a charge and draft a document so accurately that no person whatsoever could find fault with his terminology, and he knew every legal enactment off completely by heart. He rode un-ostentatiously dressed in a coat of varied colours, around which was a silk girdle with small ornamental bands. I shall tell you no more about his dress.

A Franklin (a wealthy landowner), who had a beard as white as a daisy and a ruddy complexion, kept him company. In the morning he loved a cake soaked in wine, for it was his delight to pursue a life of pleasure. Indeed, he was the true disciple of Epicurus, the philosopher who held the opinion that happiness was the chief good of life. He was an important head of a household and acted like Saint Julian in his own country. Apart from the fact that his bread and ale were always of the same high standard, I can assure you that no one kept a better cellar than he.

His household never lacked roast meat. He had such a plentiful supply of fish and flesh that his establishment abounded with meat and drink and all kinds of delicacies. According to the various seasons of the year he changed his food and meals and kept a large number of partridges fattening in coops and many bream and pike in his fish-pond. There was trouble for his cook if his sauce was not highly spiced and sharp and if his table utensils were not all pre-pared on his permanent table that usually stood ready laid in his dining hall all day long.

At sessiouns ther was he lord and sire;   355
Ful oftetyme he was knight of the shire.
An anlaas, and a gipser al of silk,
Heeng at his girdel whit as morne milk.
A shirreve hadde he been and a countour;
Was nowher such a worthy vavasour.   360

An Haberdasssher, and a Carpenter,
A Webbe, a Dyere, and a Tapicer,
Were with us eek, clothed in o liveree
Of a solempne and greet fraternitee;
Ful fressh and newe hir gere apyked was;   365
Hir knyves were y-chaped noght with bras,
But al with silver, wroght ful clene and weel,
Hire girdles and hir pouches everydeel.
Wel seemed ech of hem a fair burgeys
To sitten in a yeldhalle on a deys.   370
Everich for the wisdom that he can
Was shaply for to been an alderman;
For catel hadde they ynogh and rente;
And eek hir wyves wolde it wel assente;
And elles certeyn were they to blame.   375
It is ful fair to been y-cleped *Madame*,
And goon to vigilies al bifore,
And have a mantel roialliche y-bore.

A Cook they hadde with hem for the nones,
To boille the chiknes with the marybones,   380
And poudre-marchant tart and galingale;
Wel coude he knowe a draughte of London ale;
He coude rooste and sethe and broille and frye,
Maken mortreux and wel bake a pye.
But greet harm was it, as it thoughte me,   385
That on his shinne a mormal hadde he;
For blankmanger, that made he with the beste.

A Shipman was ther, wonynge fer by weste;
For aught I woot he was of Dertemouthe.
He rood upon a rouncy as he couthe,   390
In a gowne of faldyng to the knee.
A daggere hangynge on a laas hadde he
Aboute his nekke under his arm adoun.
The hoote somer hadde maad his hewe al broun;

He was president during the sessions of the law courts and quite frequently he had been the Knight of the Shire. He had a knife and a purse, completely of silk, hanging from his belt which was as white as the morning milk. He had also served as a sheriff and an auditor, and nowhere was there such an excellent squire.

There were also a Haberdasher, a Carpenter, a Clothweaver, a Dyer, and an Upholsterer, all of whom were clothed in the distinctive dress of an important and powerful religious guild. Their clothing had been freshly and recently trimmed, while their knives were completely mounted with silver instead of the usual brass, beautifully and finely wrought, and their belts and purses were done entirely in the same way. All of them seemed to be men of substance who were fit to sit on a dais in a Guildhall. All of them had sufficient knowledge, property and income to have been aldermen of their boroughs; and surely their wives would have been at fault if they would not willingly agree to it! How pleasant it is to be called 'My Lady', leading the way to the vigils, and have one's train carried like a queen!

They had brought a Cook with them just for the occasion so that he could boil chickens with their marrow-bones, sharp seasoning powder and aromatic root. He was not slow in recognizing a draught of London ale and knew how to roast, steam, boil and fry, make stews and bake a pie nicely. To me, however, it seemed a great pity that he had a cancerous sore on his skin. As for honey and rice, well, he could cook that with the best.

There was a Shipman who dwelt far in the West and, possibly, he hailed from Dartmouth. With a dagger which hung from a lanyard stretching from his neck to his arm and dressed in a gown of coarse cloth reaching to the knee he rode awkwardly, as well as he was able upon a hack. The fierce sun had made his complexion quite brown.

And certeinly he was a good felawe.   395
Ful many a draughte of wyn had he i-drawe
From Burdeux ward, whil that the chapman sleep;
Of nyce conscience took he no keep.
If that he faught, and hadde the hyer hond,
By water he sente hem hoom to every lond.   400
But of his craft to rekene wel his tydes,
His stremes and his daungers him bisydes,
His herberwe and his moone, his lodemenage,
Ther nas noon swich from Hulle to Cartage.
Hardy he was, and wys to undertake;   405
With many a tempest hadde his berd been shake:
He knew wel alle the havenes, as they were,
From Gootland to the Cape of Fynystere,
And every cryke in Bretayne and in Spayne.
His barge y-cleped was the Maudelayne.   410

   With us ther was a Doctour of Phisyk;
In all this world ne was ther noon him lyk,
To speke of phisyk and of surgerye;
For he was grounded in astronomye.
He kepte his pacient a ful greet deel   415
In houres by his magik natureel.
Wel coude he fortunen the ascendent
Of his ymages for his pacient.
He knew the cause of everich maladye—
Were it of hoot, or cold, or moyste, or drye—   420
And where they engendred and of what humour;
He was a verray, parfit practisour.

The cause y-knowe and of his harm the roote,
Anon he yaf the sike man his boote.
Ful redy hadde he his apothecáries   425
To sende him drogges and his letuáries,
For ech of hem made oother for to wynne—
Hir frendshipe nas nat newe to bigynne.
   Wel knew he the olde Esculapius
And Deiscorides, and eek Rufus,   430
Olde Ypocras, Haly and Galien,
Serapion, Razis and Avicen,
Averrois, Damascien and Constantyn,
Bernard and Gatesden and Gilbertyn.

Although I feel he was a good fellow, he had stolen many a draught of wine on the voyage home from Bordeaux while the merchant was sleeping. He did not worry about a clear conscience. If he took part in a fight and gained the upper hand, he threw his victims overboard. When it came to estimating the tides, the currents, the perils facing him, his harbourage, the phases of the moon and pilotage, no one from Hull to Carthage could be compared with him. He was both courageous and prudent in his undertakings. Although his beard had been shaken by many a storm, he knew all the harbours that existed from Gothland to Cape Finisterre and every creek in Brittany and Spain. His barque was called 'The Magdalene'.

A Doctor of Medicine was with us too. In the realm of medicine and surgery there was no one anywhere like him for he had been well-instructed in astrology. In hours of the greatest planetary influence he tended his patient very conscientiously by means of astrology and could say when the rising planets corresponding to his talismans were favourable. He knew the origin of every illness, whether it was hot or cold, moist or dry, where the maladies began and of what kind they were. I tell you he was a good practitioner.

Once the cause and the root of the trouble were diagnosed, he prescribed the remedy for the sick man immediately. In the meantime he had his druggists always ready to send him drugs and medicinal powders, for they gave trade to each other and their friendship had been long established.

He was well acquainted with old Aesculapius, Dioscorides, Rufus, old Hippocrates, Alhazen, Galen, Serapion, Rhazes, Avicenna, Averroes, Damascien, Constantius Afer, Bernard Gordon, John Gatesden and Gilbertus Anglicus.

Of his diete mesurable was he,   435
For it was of no superfluitee,
But of greet norissyng and digestíble.
His studie was but litel on the Bible.
In sangwyn and in pers he clad was al,
Lyned with taffata and with sendal.   440
And yet he was but esy of dispence;
He kepte that he wan in pestilence:
For gold in phisik is a cordial,
Therefore he lovede gold in special.

   A good Wyf was ther of bisyde Bathe,   445
But she was som-del deef and that was scathe.
Of clooth-makyng she hadde swich an haunt
She passed hem of Ypres and of Gaunt.
In al the parisshe wyf ne was ther noon
That to the offrynge bifore hire sholde goon,   450
And if ther dide, certeyn so wrooth was she,
That she was out of alle charitee.
Hir coverchiefs ful fyne were of ground:
I dorste swere they weyeden ten pound,
That on a Sonday were upon hir heed.   455
Hir hosen weren of fyn scarlet reed
Ful streite y-teyd, and shoes ful moyste and newe;
Boold was hir face and fair and of reed hewe.

   She was a worthy womman al hir lyve;
Housbondes at chirche dore she hadde fyve,   460
Withouten oother companye in youthe,
But ther-of nedeth nat to speke as nowthe:
And thryes hadde she been at Jerusalem;
She hadde passed many a straunge strem;
At Rome she hadde been and at Boloigne,   465
In Galice at Seint Jame, and at Coloigne;
She coude muchel of wandrynge by the weye:
Gat-tothed was she, soothly for to seye.
   Upon an amblere esily she sat,
Y-wympled wel, and on hir heed an hat   470
As brood as is a bokeler or a targe;
A foot-mantel aboute hir hipes large,
And on hir feet a paire of spores sharpe.
In felawshipe wel coude she laughe and carpe;
Of remedyes of love she knew perchaunce,   475
For she coude of that art the olde daunce.

He ate but sparingly but what he did eat was very nourishing and digestible. Very rarely did he read the Bible. Although he was dressed completely in a scarlet and bluish-grey cloth lined with taffeta and silk, his expenditure was moderate and he saved what he earned in time of plague, because after all gold is a heart-tonic in medicine, and so he loved gold above all things.

Again, there was a good Wife from near Bath but it was a pity that she was somewhat deaf for she possessed so much skill in cloth-weaving that she even excelled the weavers of Ypres and Ghent. No woman in the whole parish dared to take precedence of her when going to the offertory, and indeed, if anyone did, she became so angry that she lost all self-control. The head-dresses that she wore on Sundays were of an exquisite pattern – I dare say they weighed ten pounds—; her tightly-fastened stockings were a bright scarlet; and her shoes were supple and of the latest fashion. She had a bold, attractive face with a ruddy complexion.

As she had been an attractive woman all her life, she had accompanied five husbands to the Church door, without mentioning the company she kept in her youth but there is no point in making comments about that at present. She had been to Jerusalem three times and had crossed many a foreign river. She had also visited Rome, Bologna, the shrine of St James in Galicia, and Cologne, and she knew a lot about making detours during her travels. To tell the truth, her teeth were wide apart. Wearing a wimple on her head and a hat as broad as a buckler or a shield, an over-skirt about her huge hips with a pair of sharp spurs on her feet, she sat comfortably astride an ambling horse. She was not above chattering and prattling with the rest of the company and was, perhaps, acquainted with remedies for love, for she knew the old tricks of that art.

A good man was ther of religioun,
And was a poure Persoun of a toun;
But riche he was of holy thoght and werk;
He was also a lerned man, a clerk,   480
That Cristes gospel trewely wolde preche:
Hise parisshens devoutly wolde he teche.
Benygne he was and wonder diligent,
And in adversitee ful pacient;
And swich he was y-preved ofte sythes.   485
Ful looth were him to cursen for hise tythes,
But rather wolde he yeven, out of doute,
Unto his poure parisshens aboute,
Of his offryng and eek of his substaunce:
He coude in litel thing have suffisaunce.   490
Wyd was his parisshe, and houses fer asonder,
But he ne lafte nat for reyn ne thonder.
In siknesse nor in meschief to visite
The ferreste in his parisshe, muche and lyte,
Upon his feet, and in his hand a staf.   495

  This noble ensample to his sheep he yaf,
That firste he wroghte and afterward he taughte.
Out of the gospel he tho wordes caughte,
And this figure he added eek therto,
That if gold ruste what shal iren do?   500
For if a preest be foul, on whom we truste,
No wonder is a lewed man to ruste;
And shame it is – if a preest take keep—
A shiten shepherde and a clene sheep.
Wel oghte a preest ensample for to yive   505
By his clennesse, how that his sheep sholde live.

  He sette nat his benefice to hyre
And leet his sheep encombred in the myre,
And ran to London unto Seint Poules
To seken him a chaunterie for soules,   510
Or with a bretherhed to been witholde;
But dwelte at hoom and kepte wel his folde,
So that the wolf ne made it nat miscarie;
He was a shepherde, and noght a mercenarie.

Still another was a good man of religion, a poor town Parson who, nevertheless, was rich in holy thought and work. A cleric, a learned man, he was given to preaching Christ's gospel truly and to teaching his parishioners devoutly. He had on many occasions shown himself to be kind, extremely diligent and very patient in times of trouble. He thought it hateful to excommunicate a person for not paying his tithes but rather he would doubtlessly prefer to give charity from his Easter offerings and his private property to the poor parishioners in his district. Very little was needed to give him happiness. Although his parish was large and the houses were spread far apart, he never failed, in rain or thunder, in sickness or in trouble, to visit on foot, staff in hand, both the rich and poor, even in the most distant parts of the parish.

He set a noble example to his flock by practising first what he later preached. He took these words from the Gospel and added this illustration to it – 'If gold rusts, what will happen to iron?' If a priest, in whom we trust, is evil-living, is there any wonder if an uneducated person should go astray? If a priest would take heed, he would see that it is a shame for a shepherd to be filthy but the sheep spotless, for he believed that a priest must needs set an example by his own good-living how his flock must live.

He did not let his parish out to hire and leave his sheep encumbered in the mire while he went off to St Paul's in London to seek himself a chantry for souls or to be retained by a Guild. Instead he stayed at home and took great care of his fold lest the wolf should do them harm. He was a pastor, not a hireling.

And though he holy were and vertuous,   515
He was to sinful man nat despitous,
Ne of his speche daungerous ne digne,
But in his techyng discreet and benygne;
To drawen folk to heven by fairnesse,
By good ensample, this was his bisinesse.   520
But it were any persone obstinat,
What so he were, of heigh or lowe estat,
Him wolde he snybben sharply for the nonys.
A bettre preest I trowe that nowher noon is;
He waited after no pompe and reverence,   525
Ne maked him a spiced conscience,
But Cristes lore, and his apostles twelve,
He taughte, but first he folwed it him-selve.

With him ther was a Plowman, was his brother,
That hadde y-lad of dong ful many a fother;   530
A trewe swinkere and a good was he.
Livynge in pees and parfit charitee.
God loved he best, with al his hoole herte
At alle tymes, thogh him gamed or smerte,
And thanne his neighebour right as him-selve.   535
He wolde thresshe, and therto dyke and delve,
For Cristes sake for every poure wight,
Withouten hyre, if it lay in his might.
Hise tythes payde he ful faire and wel
Bothe of his propre swink and his catel.   540
In a tabard he rood upon a mere.
  There was also a reve and a millere,
A somnour and a pardoner also,
A maunciple and myself; ther were namo.

The Millere was a stout carl for the nones,   545
Ful big he was of brawn and eek of bones;
That proved wel, for overal ther he cam
At wrastlynge he wolde have awey the ram.
He was short-sholdred, brood, a thikke knarre,
Ther nas no dore that he nolde heve of harre,   550
Or breke it at a rennyng with his heed.
  His berd, as any sowe or fox, was reed,
And therto brood, as though it were a spade.
Upon the cop right of his nose he hade
A werte, and theron stood a tuft of heres,   555
Reed as the bristles of a sowes eres;

Though he was holy and virtuous, he was neither overbearing to sinners nor domineering and proud in his speech but discreet and kind in his methods of teaching, endeavouring always to lead his people to Heaven through beauty of life and good example. If any person, however, whosoever he was, whether of high or low degree, were stubborn, he would reprove him sharply on that score. I believe there was no better priest to be found anywhere. He neither craved for pomp and deep respect nor sought to make an over-scrupulous conscience for himself. He taught the teaching of Christ and his twelve Apostles; but invariably, he first followed it himself.

With him was his brother, a Ploughman who, an honest labourer, a good man living in peace and perfect charity with all, had drawn many a cart-load of dung in his time. Whether it pleased or pained him, he loved God best with his whole heart at all times and, next to God, his neighbour even as himself. If he possibly could, he would thresh and also dig ditches and drains, for Christ's sake, for every poor person without charge, and saw to it that he paid his tithes in full punctually both by his own toil and from his own property. He rode, dressed in a smock, on a mare.

Except for a Reeve, a Miller, a Summoner, a Pardoner, a Man-ciple and myself, there were no others in the company.

The Miller was a brawny, big-boned, burly fellow at that time but his strength had stood him in good stead for he had the better of everyone everywhere and always won the prize of a ram at wrestling, while there was no door he could not heave off its hinges or break it by running at it with his head.

Short-necked, broad and thick-set, with a beard that was red like a sow's or fox's and as broad as a spade, on the very tip of his nose he had a wart on which was a tuft of hairs as red as the bristles of a sow's ears.

His nosethirles blake were and wyde;
A swerd and bokeler bar he by his syde;
His mouth as wyde was as a greet forneys.
He was a janglere and a goliardeys, 560
And that was moost of sinne and harlotryes.
Wel coude he stelen corn and tollen thryes,
And yet he hadde a thombe of gold, pardee.
A whit cote and a blew hood wered he;
A baggepipe wel coude he blowe and sowne, 565
And therwithal he broghte us out of town.

A gentil Maunciple was ther of a temple,
Of which achatours mighte take exemple
For to be wyse in byynge of vitaille;
For, whether that he payde or took by taille, 570
Algate he wayted so in his achaat
That he was ay biforn and in good staat.
Now is nat that of God a ful fair grace
That swich a lewed mannes wit shal pace
The wisdom of an heep of lerned men? 575
Of maistres hadde he mo than thryes ten,
That were of lawe expert and curious,
Of which ther were a duzeyne in that hous
Worthy to been stywardes of rente and lond
Of any lord that is in Engelond, 580
To make him live by his propre good
In honour dettelees, but he were wood,
Or live as scarsly as him list desire,
And able for to helpen al a shire
In any caas that mighte falle or happe; 585
And yet this Maunciple sette hir aller cappe.

The Reve was a sclendre colerik man.
His berd was shave as ny as ever he can,
His heer was by his eres ful round y-shorn,
His tope was dokked lyk a preest biforn; 590
Ful longe were his legges and ful lene,
Y-lyk a staf, there was no calf y-sene.
Wel coude he kepe a gerner and a bynne,
Ther was noon auditour coude of him wynne,
Wel wiste he, by the droghte, and by the reyn, 595
The yeldynge of his seed and of his greyn.

His nostrils black and wide, his mouth as large as a huge furnace, he carried a sword and a buckler by his side. He was a quarrelsome and foul-mouthed fellow whose chattering was concerned with immorality and dirty stories. Though he knew well how to steal corn and take three times the toll due, yet he was a good judge of that grain. He wore a white coat and blue hood. He was very skilled in playing the bagpipes and led us out of town to their music.

There was also a charming Manciple of an Inn of Court, from whom purchasers could take an example on how to be prudent in buying provisions, for, whether he paid cash or bought on credit, at any rate he was so careful in his purchasing that he was always on time and had cash in hand. Surely it is a very good gift of God that the intelligence of such an uneducated man can keep pace with a crowd of learned people. Although he was employed by more than thirty men who were expert and skilled in the law, there were a dozen in that establishment who were themselves fit to be the stewards of income and property of any lord in England. Not only could they have seen to it that their lord, of course, that is unless he was out of his senses, could live honourably, free from debt, on his own income but they could also have arranged it for him to live as economically as he wished. They were also capable of helping anyone in the Shire in any lawsuit that might come about. Despite all this, this Manciple made fools of them all.

The Reeve was a slim, bad-tempered man whose beard was shaved as closely as possible, his hair cut around his ears and that on the crown of his head tonsured like a priest's. His legs were long and lanky just like walking-sticks and his calves were not visible.

He had so much experience in taking care of a granary and a bin that no auditor could get the better of him. He estimated, according to whether it had been a dry or a wet season, the yield of his seed and grain.

His lordes sheep, his neet, his dayerye,
His swyn, his hors, his stoor, and his pultrye,
Was hoolly in this Reves governyng,
And by his covenant yàf the rekenyng   600
Syn that his lord was twenty yeer of age;
Ther coude no man bringe him in arrerage.
Ther nas baillif, ne herde, nor oother hyne,
That he ne knew his sleighte and his covyne;
They were adrad of him as of the deeth.   605
  His wonyng was ful fair upon an heeth,
With grene trees y-shadwed was his place.
He coude bettre than his lord purchace.
Ful riche he was a-stored prively;
His lord wel coude he plesen subtilly   610
To yeve and lene hym of his owne good
And have a thank, and yet a cote and hood.

  In youthe he hadde lerned a good mister,
He was a wel good wrighte, a carpentér.
This Reve sat upon a ful good stot   615
That was al pomely grey and highte Scot;
A long surcote of pers upon he hade,
And by his syde he bar a rusty blade.
  Of Northfolk was this Reve of which I telle,
Bisyde a toun men clepen Baldeswelle.   620
Tukked he was, as is a frere, aboute,
And evere he rood the hyndreste of our route.

  A Somnour was ther with us in that place,
That hadde a fyr-reed cherubinnes face,
For sawcefleem he was, with eyen narwe.   625
As hoot he was and lecherous as a sparwe,
With scalled browes blake and piled berd;
Of his visage children were aferd.
Ther nas quiksilver, lítarge, ne brimstoon,
Boras, ceruce, ne oille of tartre noon,   630
Ne oynement that wolde clense and byte,
That hym might helpen of his whelkes whyte,
Nor of the knobbes sittynge on his chekes.
Wel loved he garleek, oynons, and eek lekes,
And for to drinken strong wyn, reed as blood,   635
Than wolde he speke and crye as he were wood.
And whan that he wel dronken hadde the wyn,
Than wolde he speke no word but Latyn.

In addition, his lord's sheep, his cattle, his dairy produce, his swine, his horses, his stock, his poultry, all were completely under the management of this Reeve and, by agreement, he had supplied the estimates ever since his lord was twenty years old. No one could ever accuse him of being a defaulter. He was aware of the cunning and fraud that every bailiff, every herdsman, and every other servant was liable to practise and they were as frightened of him as the plague.

His dwelling was pleasantly situated upon a heath and was shaded with green trees. As he could make purchases more shrewdly than his lord, he had amassed on the quiet great wealth. In a cunning way he could please his lord by giving and lending him even from his own property and still earn his thanks and be rewarded with a coat and hood for it as well.

As a youth he had learnt a useful trade and had been a good carpenter. Seated on a very fine cob, dappled grey and called Scot, he wore a long overcoat of bluish-grey cloth and carried a rusty sword by his side. This person about whom I am speaking lived in the town of Baldswell in Norfolk. His coat tucked into his girdle just like a friar's he was always in the rear of our company.

With us in that company was a Summoner who had small eyes and the fiery red face of a cherub, covered with pimples. He was violent and as lustful as a sparrow in his conduct and had scabby, black eyebrows and a scanty beard. The children were scared of his face. No mercury, litharge, sulphur, borax, white lead ointment, cream of tartar or any other ointment could be obtained to cleanse and cauterise him nor was there any to cure his white pimples or the pustules that disfigured his cheeks. He loved garlic, onions and leeks passionately and was very fond of strong, blood-red wine. Under its influence he would talk and shout as if he had lost his senses but, when he had taken a good draught of wine, he spoke nothing but Latin.

A fewe termes hadde he, two or thre,
That he had lerned out of som decree—
No wonder is, he herde it al the day;
And eek ye knowen wel how that a jay
Can clepen *Watte* as wel as kan the pope.
But whoso coude in oother thing him grope,
Thanne hadde he spent al his philosophye;
Ay *Questio quid juris* wolde he crye.
  He was a gentil harlot and a kynde;
A bettre felawe sholde men noght fynde.
He wolde suffre for a quart of wyn
A good felawe to have his concubyn
A twelf month, and excuse him atte fulle;

Ful prively a fynch eek coude he pulle.
And if he fond owher a good felawe,
He wolde techen him to have noon awe,
In swich caas, of the erchedeknes curs,
But-if a mannes soule were in his purs;
For in his purs he sholde y-punisshed be:
'Purs is the erchedeknes helle,' seyde he.
But wel I woot he lyed right in dede;
Of cursyng oghte ech gilty man him drede—
For curs wol slee, right as assoillyng saveth—
And also war him of a *Significavit*.
  In daunger hadde he at his owne gyse
The yonge girles of the diocyse,
And knew hir counseil, and was al hir reed.
A gerland hadde he set upon his heed,
As greet as it were for an ale-stake;
A bokeler hadde he maad him of a cake.

  With him ther was a gentil Pardoner
Of Rouncival, his freend and his compeer,
That streight was comen fro the court of Rome.
Ful loude he song, *Com hider, love, to me*.
This somnour bar to him a stif burdoun,
Was never trompe of half so greet a soun.
  This Pardoner hadde heer as yelow as wex,
But smothe it heng, as dooth a strike of flex;
By ounces henge his lokkes that he hadde,
And therwith he his shuldres overspradde;
But thinne it lay, by colpons, oon and oon;

640

645

650

655

660

665

670

675

He knew two or three legal phrases which he had learnt from some statute, which is not to be wondered at for he used to hear them all day long. You know well how a jay can repeat 'Walter' as well as the Pope. If, however, anyone had questioned him about anything else, then it would be found that he had exhausted all his knowledge and would keep on saying, 'Which part of the law applies?'

Although he was a good-natured and kind type of rascal, you could never find a bigger rogue. For a quart of wine he would forgive any disreputable scoundrel completely for keeping his concubine for a year.

Secretly he knew how to plunder a fool and, if he met a person of doubtful character, he would instruct him that, unless his soul resided in his purse, he need not be afraid of the archdeacon's power of excommunication, for he would only be punished by a heavy bribe. He maintained, 'The purse is the archdeacon's power of excommunication.' For my part, I know that, in fact, he lied, for every guilty man should fear excommunication because excommunication will slay even as the Absolution will save. I advise him to beware of a 'Significavit'.

In his own way he had all the young people of the diocese in his power and, as he was their adviser in everything, he knew all their secrets. He wore on his forehead a garland that would have been large enough for an inn-sign and he had made himself a buckler from a loaf of bread.

Alongside him rode his close friend, a noble Pardoner from Roncesvalles, who had come straight from the court of Rome and who sang, 'Come hither, my love, to me' at the top of his voice, the Summoner accompanying him with such a strong droning bass that a trumpet could never make half as much noise.

The Pardoner's wax coloured hair hung smoothly like a hank of flax and fell in bunches of thin locks which spread down over his shoulders.

But hood, for jolitee, he wered noon,   680
For it was trussed up in his walet.
Him thoughte he rood al of the newe jet;
Dischevele, save his cappe, he rood al bare.
Swiche glarynge eyen hadde he as an hare.
A vernicle hadde he sowed upon his cappe;   685
His walet lay biforn him in his lappe
Bret-ful of pardon, come from Rome all hoot.
    A voys he hadde as smal as hath a goot;
No berd hadde he, ne never sholde have,
As smothe it was as it were late y-shave;   690
I trowe he were a geldyng or a mare.

    But of his craft, fro Berwyk unto Ware,
Ne was ther swich another pardoner,
For in his male he hadde a pilwe-beer,
Which that, he seyde, was Oure Lady veyl;   695
He seyde he hadde a gobet of the seyl
That Sëint Peter hadde whan that he wente
Upon the see till Jhesu Crist him hente.
He hadde a croys of latoun ful of stones,
And in a glas he hadde pigges bones.   700
But with thise relikes, whan that he fond
A poure person dwellynge up on lond,
Upon a day he gat him more moneye
Than that the person gat in monthes tweye;
And thus with feyned flaterye and japes   705
He made the person and the peple his apes.
But, trewely to tellen atte laste,
He was in chirche a noble ecclesiaste;
Wel coude he rede a lessoun or a storie,
But alderbest he song an offertorie,   710
For wel he wiste, whan that song was songe,
He moste preche and wel affyle his tonge
To wynne silver, as he ful wel coude;
Therefore he song so merily and loude.

    Now have I toold you shortly in a clause   715
The staat, tharray, the nombre, and eek the cause
Why that assembled was this companye
In Southwerk at this gentil hostelrye,
That highte the Tabard, faste by the Belle.

From personal caprice he wore no hood but carried it in his bag for it seemed more festive to him to ride bare-headed, save for a cap, on which he had sewn a copy of St Veronica's handkerchief. His eyes glared like a hare's and his voice was as small as a goat's. As he had just lately come back from Rome, he had a bag, brimful of pardons, all hot and ready for sale, hanging in front of him on his lap. He had no beard nor was he likely to have one, as his chin was as smooth as if it had only just been shaved. Indeed, I believe he was a gelded horse or a mare.

But there was no other pardoner from Berwick to Ware like him in the profession, for he carried in his bag a pillowcase, which, so he claimed, was Our Lady's veil. He declared that he had a piece of the sail belonging to the ship which St Peter had at the time he walked on the Sea of Galilee till Jesus Christ saved him, a cross of latten, ornamented with semi-precious stones, and the bones of a pig in a glass. When he came upon a poor parson living in a remote district, he gained for himself with these relics more money than the parson earned in two months and so, by means of false flattery and tricks, he made fools of the parson and his flock. To sum up, he was not only a capable preacher in Church but also had ability in reading a passage from the Scriptures or a legend of a Saint. Best of all he sang an offertory for he knew that, after the anthem was sung, he had to preach and use a glib tongue to gain money. He could do this excellently and so he sang cheerfully and loudly.

Now I have told you truly, in a few words, the state, the attire, the number and also the reason for this company assembling in Southwark at this excellent inn called the Tabard that was close to the Bell.

But now is tyme to you for to telle 720
How that we baren us that ilke night,
Whan we were in that hostelrye alight;
And after wol I telle of our viage
And al the remenaunt of our pilgrimage.
  But first, I pray yow of your curtesye, 725
That ye narette it nat my vileynye,
Thogh that I pleynly speke in this matere
To telle yow hir wordes and hir chere,
Ne thogh I speke hir wordes proprely,
For this ye knowen al-so wel as I, 730
Whoso shal telle a tale after a man,
He moot reherce, as ny as ever he can,
Everich a word, if it be in his charge,
Al speke he never so rudeliche and large,
Or elles he moot telle his tale untrewe, 735
Or feyne thing, or fynde wordes newe.
He may nat spare, althogh he were his brother,
He moot as wel seye o word as another.
Crist spak himself ful brode in holy writ,
And wel ye woot no vileynye is it. 740
Eek Plato seith, whoso that can him rede,
'The Wordes moote be cosyn to the dede.'
  Also I prey yow to foryeve it me
Al have I nat set folk in hir degree
Heere in this tale, as that they sholde stonde; 745
My wit is short, ye may wel understonde.

  Greet chere made oure Hoost us everichon,
And to the soper sette he us anon,
And served us with vitaille at the beste:
Strong was the wyn, and wel to drynke us leste. 750
  A semely man oure Hooste was with-alle
For to han been a marchal in an halle.
A large man he was, with eyen stepe,
A fairer burgeys was ther noon in Chepe;
Boold of his speche, and wys and wel y-taught, 755
And of manhod him lakkede right naught.
Eek therto he was right a myrie man,
And after soper pleyen he bigan,
And spak of myrthe amonges othere thinges,
Whan that we hadde maad our rekenynges; 760

It is therefore time for me to tell you how we passed our time that same night that we had arrived at the inn and then I shall describe our journey and all the rest of the pilgrimage.

First, I beg you to be courteous enough not to think me ill-bred if I speak openly about this matter, even telling you their words and about their behaviour, though I do not repeat their words accurately. For you know as well as I that anyone who wishes to repeat a story that he has heard from another must tell, if he is able, every word as faithfully as ever he can. If he is afraid of relating a story without restraint because it is too rough, then he must change his story or pretend that it is something else or even put it in fresh words. He must not spare the other person even if he were repeating his own brother's words and he must include every single word. Christ himself spoke quite openly in the Holy Scriptures and you know there is no ill-breeding contained in them. Again, Plato too says, if anyone can read him, 'The words must be related to the fact.'

I also beg you to forgive me if I have not placed the characters of this story just as they should be, according to their station in life. You will realize that my knowledge is limited.

Our Host provided good fare for every one of us, set us down to supper without more ado and served us with the very best meal, at which we took great pleasure in drinking the strong wine.

Our Host, who was fit to be a major-domo in a Guildhall, was a polite man but rather big with prominent eyes. I feel there was no more prosperous man in Cheapside. Outspoken in his speech, prudent and well-bred, he lacked none of the attributes of a man. In addition, he was a very cheerful fellow and after supper began to play music and, among other things, talked of the entertainment we should have after we had paid our accounts.

And seyde thus: 'Now, lordynges, trewely,
Ye been to me right welcome hertely;
For by my trouthe, if that I shal not lye,
I saugh nat this yeer so mery a companye
At ones in this herberwe as is now;   765
Fayn wolde I doon yow myrthe, wiste I how.
And of a myrthe I am right now bithoght,
To doon yow ese, and it shal coste noght.

   'Ye goon to Caunterbury; God yow spede,
The blisful martir quyte yow your mede!   770
And, wel I woot, as ye goon by the weye
Ye shapen yow to talen and to pleye;
For trewely confort ne myrthe is noon
To ryde by the weye doumb as a stoon;
And therfore wol I maken yow disport,   775
As I seyde erst, and doon yow som confórt.
And if you liketh alle, by oon assent,
Fór to stonden at my juggement,
And for to werken as I shal yow seye,
To-morwe, whan ye ryden by the weye,   780
Now by my fader soule that is deed,
But ye be mery, I wol yeve yow myn heed.
Hoold up your hond withouten moore speche.'

   Oure counseil was nat longe for to seche;
Us thoughte it was noght worth to make it wys,   785
And graunted him withouten more avys,
And bad him seye his verdit, as him leste.
   'Lordynges,' quod he, 'now herkneth, for the beste,
But taake it noght, I prey yow, in desdeyn;
This is the poynt, to speken short and pleyn,   790
That ech of yow to shorte with your weye
In this viage, shal telle tales tweye,
To Caunterbury ward, I mene it so,
And homward he shal tellen othere two,
Of áventures that whilom han bifalle.   795
And which of yow that berth him best of alle—
That is to seyn, that telleth in this caas
Tales of best senténce and moost solaas—
Shal have a soper at our aller cost,
Here in this place, sittynge by this post,   800
Whan that we come agayn fro Caunterbury.

'Now, gentlemen,' he said, 'on my word, you are truly right heartily welcome here, for I am not telling an untruth when I say that I have not seen this year at the same time in this lodging such a cheerful company as now. I would like to amuse you and I think I know the way. A short time ago I thought of some entertainment to cheer you up, and it will cost you nothing at all.

'May God speed you on your way to Canterbury and may the blessed martyr grant you your reward! I have learnt that you are preparing to tell stories and entertain yourselves as you go along the road; and I agree it is no comfort or fun to ride as dumb as a stone during a journey. And so, as I said just now, I shall provide some entertainment for you and see that you are cheerful. By the soul of my dead father, if you all agree unanimously to stand by my decision and do what I stipulate when you are making your journey tomorrow, I promise that you may do whatever you care with me, if I do not cheer you up. Let us have a show of hands without any further talk.'

It did not take us long to reach our decision. As we did not think it worthwhile to make it a subject of serious discussion, we agreed with him at once and bade him announce his decision whenever he pleased.

'Gentlemen,' he said, 'listen to me closely but please do not despise what I have to say. To be brief, the idea is that, to shorten this long journey, each one of you will tell two stories of adventures that once happened (I mean, of course, two on the way to Canterbury and another two on the return journey). The one who acquits himself best of all, that is to say the one who tells stories of the highest moral teaching and edification on this occasion, will win a supper at the cost of us all right here in this inn when we return from Canterbury.

And, for to make yow the moore mury,
I wol myselven gladly with yow ryde
Right at myn owne cost, and be your gyde;
And whoso wol my juggement withseye   805
Shal paye al that we spenden by the weye;
And if ye vouchesauf that it be so
Tel me anon, withouten wordes mo,
And I wol erly shape me therefore.'

  This thing was graunted, and our othes swore,   810
With ful glad herte, and preyden him also
That he would vouchesauf for to do so,
And that he wolde been our governour,
And of tales juge and reportour,
And sette a soper at a certeyn prys,   815
And we wol reuled been at his devys
In heigh and lowe; and thus by oon assent
We been acorded to his juggement.
And therupon the wyn was fet anon;
We dronken and to reste wente echon   820
Withouten any lenger taryynge.

  Amorwe, whan that day gan for to springe,
Up roos oure Hoost and was oure aller cok,
And gadrede us togidre alle in a flok,
And forth we riden, a litel more than paas,   825
Unto the wateryng of Saint Thomas;
And ther our Hoost bigan his hors areste
And seyde, 'Lordynges, herkneth, if yow leste!
Ye woot your foreward and I it yow recorde.
If even-song and morwe-song accorde,   830
Lat se now who shal telle the firste tale.
As ever mote I drynke wyn or ale,
Whoso be rebel to my juggement
Shal paye for al that by the way is spent.
Now draweth cut, er that we ferrer twinne.   835
He which that hath the shorteste shal biginne.
Sire Knight,' quod he, 'my maister and my lord,
Now draweth cut, for that is myn accord.
Cometh neer,' quod he, 'my lady Prioresse,
And ye, sir Clerk, lat be your shamefastnesse,   840
Ne studieth noght; ley hond to, every man.'

To cheer you all the more, I shall myself gladly ride with you, pay my own expenses and act as your guide. If anyone disputes my decision, then he will have to pay all our incidental expenses. If you are willing for this agreement to stand, tell me at once, without any further discussion, and I shall straightaway prepare myself to that end.'

This proposal was adopted and we swore oaths to that effect in a cheerful manner. We also invited him to act as he had proposed, namely that he should be our leader, the judge and critic of our stories, and that he should arrange a supper at a definite price and then we should obey him in everything. And so we unanimously bound ourselves to his decision and the wine was fetched at once. We had a drink and everyone went to bed without dawdling any longer.

When dawn came the next morning, our Host arose before us all and, collecting us together in a company, we rode forth at hardly more than walking pace to St Thomas's Well. Here our Host stopped his horse and said, 'Gentlemen, listen to me please. Although you probably remember your agreement, I shall remind you of it. If you agree this morning with what you said last evening, let us decide who will tell the first story. By my intention never to drink anything except wine or ale, the one who will not obey my decision will pay for everything that we spend during the journey. Now, let us draw lots before we go any farther. The person who draws the shortest straw will begin. Sir Knight, my lord and master,' he continued, 'take your draw as I say. Come nearer, my Lady Prioress, and you, Sir Clerk, don't be shy. Don't stand there day-dreaming. Let us all begin.'

Anon to drawen every wight bigan,
And, shortly for to tellen as it was,
Were it by aventure, or sort, or cas,
The sothe is this, the cut fil to the Knight,   845
Of which ful blithe and glad was every wight:
And telle he moste his tale as was resoun
By foreward and by composicioun,
As ye han herd; what nedeth wordes mo?
And whan this gode man saugh it was so,   850
As he that wys was and obedient
To kepe his foreward by his free assent,
He seyde, 'Sin I shal beginne the game,
What, welcome be the cut, a Goddes name!
Now let us ryde, and herkneth what I seye.'   855
And with that word we riden forth our weye,
And he bigan with right a myrie chere
His tale anon, and seyde in this manere.

Straightaway every one came forward for the draw and, to be brief, whether it was by luck, chance or fortune, the fact is that the lot fell upon the Knight. This pleased every one immensely, and he had to tell his story, as was right, according to our agreed decision, as you have heard. Need I say more? When the gentleman saw that it was so, like one who is wise and obedient in keeping to his agreement, he said, 'Since I must begin the entertainment, in God's name, let the draw be welcome! Now let us ride forward and listen to what I shall say.'

With these words we rode forth on our journey and the Knight began to tell his story in a right happy manner at once and related it thus.

Chaucer's grammar

It should not be forgotten that, in point of time, Chaucer stands about midway between the days of King Alfred, who died in 899, and our own. We would therefore expect the language he wrote to represent a transitional stage between Old English and Modern English, and this is in fact what we find. There were a number of quite distinct dialects of Middle English in Chaucer's time, and it was partly owing to his prestige that his own speech gained ultimately the mastery; that, and the importance of London. Old English (sometimes still called Anglo-Saxon) was a fully inflected language, closely resembling Modern German in the variety and complexity of its terminations. Modern English has very few inflections, and those it has are very simple to learn. Chaucer's inflections are far fewer than those of King Alfred, though more than our own. What we shall see is that a very large number of the inflections of Old English are represented in Chaucer by the single letter -e, which is as a rule pronounced; in Modern English we often write the -e but do not pronounce it. This is not a complete account of Chaucerian inflection, but it will be a guide to much of his grammar and much of his versification. Some of the inflections in Old English were made by changing the root vowels in both nouns and verbs, and these changes are mostly preserved in Chaucer. But even so, as early as the poet's time, there was a tendency to get rid of irregular or anomalous forms, and to require all words to conform to pattern. We shall now indicate the normal accidence of Middle English as shown in Chaucer's work; the abnormalities will be pointed out in the notes on particular words.

Nouns

There is no standard termination for the nominative and accusative singular. The dative singular is unchanged or ends in -e, and all other cases, singular and plural, end in -es. As sometimes the nominative and accusative end in -e, it must be remembered that a final -e is not a sure sign of the dative singular of a noun. Sometimes also the -es becomes -s in a long word.

Some words have plurals in -en or -n; these are survivals of Old English nouns which had plurals in -an; we still have 'oxen' in Modern English, and a few others.

Prepositions all take the dative case.

Adjectives

A few adjectives end normally in -e in the nominative and accusative singular, but most end in a consonant. In the plural all adjectives end in -e. But when an adjective is preceded by a demonstrative or a possessive adjective, such as 'the', 'his', 'your', it has an -e in all cases, both singular and plural. This form in -e is called the 'weak' form; the uninflected singular is called 'strong'.

The comparatives end in -er, and the superlatives in -este. The ancestors of the modern irregular comparisons are, naturally, found in Chaucer.

Pronouns

These are so like the Modern English pronouns that we shall not need to say much about them. We shall not, however, find forms corresponding to our 'its', 'their' and 'them'. Instead we shall find 'his' used for persons and things, 'hir' (which is easily confused with 'hir', which means 'her') and 'hem' respectively. Sometimes the pronoun 'thou' is attached to the verb when used in an interrogative sentence. We find 'maistow' for 'mayst thou'.

The plural of 'that' is 'tho', not 'those'.

The relatives show the greatest differences from the modern pronouns. Our 'who' is not relative in Chaucer, but interrogative. We find that 'that' is the chief relative if followed by 'he', 'his' or 'him' after an interval of a few words. 'That . . . he' will be translated by 'who'; 'that . . . his' by 'whose'; and 'that . . . him' by 'whom'. 'Whiche' is used as a relative in the singular and plural, for persons and things. We still say: 'Our Father, Which art in Heaven . . .'. 'Whose' and 'whom' can be used as relatives, although 'who' cannot. 'Which?' means 'of what kind?' When 'what' is used interrogatively it means 'why?'

The chief indefinite pronoun is 'man', or 'men'. It acts like the French *on* (or the German *man*), and should as a rule be translated by 'one', 'anyone'.

Verbs

These are either strong or weak, according to the method of formation of the past tense and past participle (again as in German). Change of vowel characterizes a strong verb; addition of -ede, -de or -te to form past tense, and of -ed, -d or -t to form past participle indicates a weak verb.

The conjugations of typical strong and weak verbs are shown below.

		Strong: to singen	Weak: to maken
Indic. pres. singular	1	singe	make
	2	singest	makest
	3	singeth	maketh
plural 1,2,3		singe(n)	make(n)

Subj. pres.	singular	1	singe	make
		2	singe	make
		3	singe	make
	plural	1,2,3	singe(n)	make(n)

Indic. past	singular	1	song, sang	made
		2	song(e)	madest
		3	song, sang	made, maked
	plural	1,2,3	songe(n)	made(n), makede(n)

Subj. past	singular	1	songe	made
		2	songe	made
		3	songe	made
	plural	1,2,3	songe(n)	made(n)

| Imperative | Singular | sing | make |
| | Plural | singeth, singe | maketh, make |

| Participles | Present | singing(e) | making(e) |
| | Past | ysonge(n) | ymaked, maad |

| Infinitive | Present | sing(n) | make (n) |

There is a tendency for a final -n to drop off.

Adverbs

Many adverbs resemble the weak adjective, having the -e ending; others add -ly or -liche to the adjective. Those in the first group lose their -e eventually, and give us the phenomenon of adjectives and adverbs of the same form in Modern English: e.g. He runs fast, He is a fast runner.

Chaucer's pronunciation and versification

Pronunciation

Chaucer's English is the East Midland dialect. For a considerable time before the Conquest the language of government and literature had been West Saxon, the dialect of King Alfred's capital, Winchester. After the Conquest the French language predominated in ruling, educated and, therefore, literary circles, the various dialects of English being restricted to the uneducated. Gradually, however, in the fourteenth century the English language took over from the French language as the language of state, government and literature, and it was the East Midland dialect of London and the Home Counties, where lay the seats of court, government and the universities, that became the standard.

This Standard English was the combination of the Old English, or Anglo-Saxon, and French, and this is reflected in Chaucer's vocabulary and pronunciation. In Chaucer we find the beginning of English literature as we now know it; the acceptance of an English language, with Saxon and French words blended into an 'English tongue', understood by all people. Chaucer's works were probably intended to be read aloud to an audience – at Court or to friends. If we can learn to read Chaucer with as near the original pronunciation as possible, the wit, beauty and humour will become clearer; and at the same time the meaning of many of those words made difficult for us by archaic spelling will be clarified. A good guide is to pronounce the words of French origin as if they were French, and words of Anglo-Saxon origin as if they were German.

It would be easier, and more fun, to learn the pronunciation of Chaucer's English by listening to gramophone records of

Chaucer's poetry in what is considered to be the original pronunciation. Several recordings have been made of modern scholars reading Chaucer. We particularly recommend the reading of the Prologue to The Canterbury Tales (Argo, PLP 1001) mentioned at the end of the Bibliography, p. 6. However, it will be helpful to study the following table, which indicates approximately Chaucer's pronunciation:

Vowels

Words of English origin

Short vowels

'a' pronounced like 'a' in French *placer*; but not like 'a' in English 'cat'.

'e' pronounced like 'e' in Modern English 'men'.

'i' pronounced like 'i' in 'pin'. 'y' is often written for 'i', and has the same sound as 'i'.

'o' pronounced like 'o' in 'not'. Before letters written with a number of short strokes, like 'm, n', and especially a combination of these two, 'o' is written for 'u', but should be prolounced like 'u', as for example, in 'comen, love, somer, monk'.

'u' pronounced like 'u' in 'pull', or like 'oo' in 'soot'; but not like 'u' in 'duke'.

Long vowels

It is often possible to recognize a long vowel by its being duplicated in writing. For example 'taak' contains a long 'a';

'sooth' contains a long 'o'.

'a' pronounced like 'a' in 'father'.

'e' pronounced like 'e' acute or like 'e' grave in French. Only a knowledge of the origin of the words in Old English can guide the reader to distinguish between the close and open sounds, as they are called, in Chaucer; but the former sound is usually represented in Modern English by 'ee', and the latter by 'ea'. Modern English 'need' had a close vowel in Old English, where it was spelt 'nēd'; Modern English 'mead', a meadow, was 'mēd' in Old English with an open vowel. As an indication that these two vowels had distinct sounds, we may note that Chaucer very rarely makes them rhyme.

'i' (often written 'y'), pronounced like 'ee' in 'feel'.

'o' pronounced either like 'o' in 'so', or like 'a' in 'call'. Chaucer recognizes the different pronunciations just as he distinguishes the two long 'e' sounds. In Modern English the former sound is represented by 'oo', as in 'soon' while the latter is like the vowel sound in 'note'.

'u' pronounced like 'oo' in 'soon'.

Diphthongs

'ai, ei, ay' and 'ey' pronounced like the dipthong in 'day', though some authorities believe they were sounded like 'i' in 'line'.

'au, aw' pronounced like 'ou' in 'house'; but before the combination '-ght' like the 'o' in 'not'.

'eu, ew' pronounced like 'ew' in 'few'.

'oi, oy' pronounced like 'oy' in 'boy'.

'ou, ow' pronounced like 'u', or like 'au, aw'.

In words of French origin

Such of these words as had already become part and parcel of the everyday speech would obey the rules for the pronunciation of English vowel sounds; the others would retain the vowels of the French language, which were sounded much as they are today.

In unaccented syllables

The final '-e' so common at the end of a line and elsewhere is sounded like the second syllable of the word 'china'.

Consonants

The consonants had generally the same pronunciation as they have today, with certain slight modifications.

There were no silent consonants, unless, as some scholars believe, the 'g' before 'n' is not sounded.

'kn' is pronounced as in Modern German.

'gg' is pronounced like the 'dge' in Modern English 'ridge'.

'gh' as in Modern German may be either palatal or guttural, according to whether it is preceded by a palatal or a guttural vowel.

'ng' is sounded as in southern English 'fin-ger', not as in 'sing-er'.

'th' (initial) is sounded as in 'thin', not as in 'then'.

'ch' in words of both English and French origin is pronounced like the 'ch' of Modern English 'choose'.

'w' before 'r' is pronounced like a rapidly sounded 'oo'.

'h' in words of French origin and in words like 'he, him', which are rarely emphasized, is silent; but in most words of English origin an initial 'h' is sounded. Where the metre demands that a final '-e' should be elided before an 'h', that 'h' is silent.

Final 'f' is sounded as 'f', and not as 'v'.

Final 's' is sounded as 's', and not as 'z'.

Chaucer's use of the final -e

It is important to say something about the function of the final -e found at the end of many words in Chaucer's verse. At the beginning of the fourteenth century these were generally sounded as separate syllables, but by the end of the century they were coming into disuse. In Chaucer's verse the final -e may represent an inflexional change in a noun, an adjective, or a verb; or it may be what is left of a word-ending in Old English. There are many explanations of this termination, and the following rules usually apply in Chaucer:

1 The final -e is usually sounded, except when
(a) it is slurred over before a word beginning with a vowel (e.g. Of deerne love he koudeand of solas): before certain words beginning with 'h'; any part of the verb to have (e.g. a clerk-hadde litherly biset his while); the adverbs heer, how, and a silent 'h' as in honour, him and hem (e.g. For for no cry hir maide koudehim calle).
(b) it is sometimes dropped in some words in common use as were, wolde.

2 The final -e should always be sounded at the end of a line.

Versification

It is important to know how to read Chaucer's verse, for it was to a great extent through ignorance of how the verses scanned that even a great critic like Dryden called Chaucer a 'rude rhymer'. He was really a very finished artist.

We have already indicated how the words were pronounced, and a frequent hearing of the records made by

Professor H. C. Wyld will have helped to impress this pronunciation on your mind. But something remains to be said about Chaucer's metre and the way in which he has used words for poetical purposes.

The *Prologue* is written throughout in what are called heroic or decasyllabic couplets. Each line has ten syllables, normally, and the lines rhyme in pairs. The ten syllables are divided into five groups of two syllables, known as feet. In most lines an unaccented syllable begins the foot and is followed by an accented one. Such a line is No. 111:

> Upon his arm he bar a gay bracer.

A long poem written entirely in such a metre would become intolerably dull, and would necessarily induce sleep in its hearers, and it was for hearers rather than readers that Chaucer was catering. (In Corpus Christi College, Cambridge, there is a manuscript of Chaucer's *Troilus and Criseyde*, the frontispiece of which shows the poet reading to the court of Richard II.) A very common method of preventing the monotony of a long series of decasyllabic lines is to add an extra syllable at the end of the line, a practice found frequently in Shakespeare's later plays. Chaucer takes care to end lines with a word whose final syllable ends in an unstressed -e. An example is seen in lines 23 and 24:

> At nyght was come into that hostlerye
> Wel nine and twenty in a compaignye

where each line of the couplet has eleven syllables, the last being an unstressed -e. Often the final syllable is -es, as in lines 11 and 12:

> So priketh hem nature in hir corages
> Than longen folk to goon on pilgrimages.

Another variant is seen in line 76, where he has nine syllables only, the unstressed syllable of the first foot being omitted:

> Ál bismotered with his habergeon

The very first line of the *Prologue* shows both omission of the first unstressed syllable, and addition of a final unstressed one:

> Whan that Áprille with his shoures soote.

In every decasyllabic line there is a pause known as a cæsura. Usually it is found near the middle of the line, that is after the fourth or fifth syllable; but Chaucer realised that the rigidity which the constant position of the pause would give to a line could be reduced by placing the cæsura elsewhere than near the middle. Hence we find that while such a line as 43:

> A Knight ther was and that a worthy man

has the pause after the fourth syllable, there are many cases of lines where it is clear that Chaucer placed the pause nearer the beginning. Line 102 halts after the third syllable, line 167 after the fourth, line 121 after the fifth, 118 after the sixth, while in 91 and 32 the cæsura comes after the seventh and eighth respectively. Chaucer's practice can be contrasted with Pope's, who took care to have his pause in the middle of his lines, and so lacks the easy rhythm of the older poet.

One other point in connection with the cæsura is to be noticed, and this is that just before a pause, Chaucer sometimes has an extra, unaccented syllable. An example is seen in line 134, where the syllable -e after *copp* is inserted before the pause preceding the word *ther*. The elision seen when two vowels come together, or one precedes a mute *h*, does not occur when the cæsural pause comes between the two vowels, or the vowel and the *h*. An example is seen at line 40.

> And whiche they were ‖ and of what degree

where the -e of *were* would regularly have been elided before the a of *and*. All these departures from a rigid standard have the effect of introducing variety into the verse, and variety brings with it gracefulness and ease, which did not characterize the works of Chaucer's contemporaries.

It will be seen that very few of the lines end in a strongly stressed syllable; most of them end in -es or in -e. This final -e is to be pronounced as the -a is pronounced in *china*. The words of French origin usually have their accent on the last syllable, as in *resoun* and *condicioun*, in lines 37 and 38, and *honour* and *courtesye* in line 46. But words which we recognize as present participles in French, like *accordaunt*, are stressed on the last syllable but one.

Textual notes

1. **whan that** When. The 'that' is like the 'que' found in French compound conjunctions, such as 'tandis que'; it cannot be translated into English.

   his This stands for both 'his' and 'its'. If you consider 'Aprille' to be personified, translate by 'his'.

   soote The same word is spelt 'swete' in line 5.

2. **perced to the roote** Pierced to the root of every plant.

3. **in swich licour, of which vertu** An awkward phrase, best translated by 'in that liquor by whose vitalizing power.' The liquor is the sap.

4. **flour** The differentiation by spelling between the meanings of 'flour' and 'flower' is comparatively recent.

5. **whan** A second clause of time is here introduced; a third begins in line 7, and a fourth in line 9; they are answered by the 'thanne' clause of line 12.

   Zephirus A personification of the west wind; 'swete', although it follows the pronominal adjective 'his', does not show the *-e* of the weak adjective, as its nominative case is also 'swete'.

7. **croppes** Not 'crops', but 'shoots'.

   yonge sonne The sun is 'young' either because the astronomical year begins with the entry of the sun into the 'Ram' on March 12th, or because the year in the Middle Ages began not on January 1st but on March 25th. 'Yonge' is an example of the weak adjective, for it follows 'the', and in the strong nominative case has no *-e*.

8. The Prologue abounds in astronomical allusions, but the astronomy of Chaucer is not that of today. The belt of the heavens which was called the Zodiac was divided into twelve equal divisions, the first of these in the astronomical year was *Aries*, the ram. It was followed by *Taurus*, the bull. The divisions of the signs of the Zodiac did not, however, correspond to the divisions of the months, and *Aries* extended from March 12th till

April 11th. Roughly half of the Ram was in April; so Chaucer means that the sun had completed its half-course of eleven days, in the Ram. The date was therefore after April 11th. As a fact, as we learn from a reference by the Host of the inn, the exact date was a week later, namely April 18th.

y-ronne The *y-* represents the usual prefix of the participle in Old English, namely *ge-*, as in modern German. You will notice again that the sound we represent by the letter *u* is frequently written as *o* by scribes of this period. This rounded letter would be easier to read in a word that contained a number of pointed letters, like *munue*.

11. **corages** Hearts. Be on your guard against giving to a Chaucerian word the meaning which corresponds to its spelling in modern English. The word is not to be translated by *courage* here. (See list of such words on page 111.)

13. **palmeres** These were pilgrims who wandered all their life through from place to place for some religious purpose or other. As time went on, these pilgrimages developed abuses, and lost their real religious significance.

16. **Engelond** Has three syllables.

17. The **martir** Was Thomas à Becket, murdered in 1170 in the Cathedral.

18. **that** Was the usual relative pronoun in Chaucer's time: *who* was an interrogative only.

17–18. Identical rhyme; *seke* and *seeke* are pronounced the same.

20. **Southwerk** Is that district of London immediately south of London Bridge. The inn then known as the 'Tabard' has gone; but a public house of the same name marks the site to the present day. The Plowman, as we are told at line 541, wore a tabard, which was a smock worn by workers; but the inn-sign probably showed a sleeveless coat, with armorial bearings, such as a herald wore.

21. **as I lay** We should say, 'where I put up'.

23. At night were come ‖ into that hostelrye.

24. **wel** The meaning must be 'just', or 'some', here.

27. **wolden** Intended to. The word is stronger in meaning than 'would'.

29. **weren esed** Were accommodated.
atte beste At the best, in the best possible manner.
atte Is *at* plus *the*, contracted.

30. **shortly** In brief, not 'before long'.
to reste At rest, set.

31. **so** In such a way. Chaucer was popular wherever he went, and had a way of getting on with people.

33. **foreward** Agreement. Again, do not use the English word of similar spelling.

34. **ther as I yow devyse** Where I describe or mention to you, namely Canterbury.

37. **me thinketh** It seems to me; do not translate by *I think*.

38. **condicioun** Standing.

40. **whiche** and **what** Are to be carefully distinguished.
whiche Means 'of what sort', like Latin *qualis*.
what Has the same meaning as at present.

41. A knight was required, under the feudal system, to do forty days' service in return for the land he 'held' from his overlord. Chaucer's Knight had obviously put in more than the required minimum of service.

43. **worthy** Respected, notable, distinguished. Do not translate by *worthy*.

44. **that fro the tyme ... he loved** The 'that' followed by 'he' was one way in which the relative pronoun could be expressed 'Who from the time ... loved chivalrous conduct'.

46. **freedom** Liberality.
curtesye Courtly behaviour.

47. **his lordes werre** The 'war' may have been the 'Hundred Years' War' or perhaps, God's war against the heathen, a kind of crusade after the Crusades proper.

48. **thereto** Moreover, in addition. It does not mean 'to that war'.

ferre Comparative of *fer*.

49. **as wel ... as** Not only ... but also.

hethenesse Heathendom. Better translated *not only in Christian lands but also in heathen*.

50. **worthinesse** Real worth.

51. It will be well to consider the campaigns of the Knight under three headings. He had fought against the Turks in the Eastern Mediterranean, against the Moors in the Western Mediterranean, and against the heathen of North-Eastern Europe, where he had a distinguished position among the Teutonic knights. Chaucer does not arrange the battles according to these groups. Alexandria, in Egypt, was taken by the Christian knights under the King of Cyrpus in 1365; other notable engagements in this war are mentioned in lines 58 and 65.

52. To begin the board, or take the head of the table, was a signal honour. It was assigned to the most distinguished knight in the company, who was virtually the president.

53. **Pruce** The Teutonic knights were founded in Palestine, but had been fighting in Poland to drive off the heathen of Lithuania and of Prussia.

54. **Lettow** Lithuania.

Ruce Russian.

56. **Gernade** Granada, the southern kingdom of the Moors in Spain, of which Algeciras was the southernmost fortress. It fell to the King of Castile in 1344.

57. **Belmarye** Part of Morocco, and then allied to the Moors of Granada, now Belmarin.

58. **Lyeys** Now Ayas.

Satalye Adalia. These were important ports on the southern coast of Asia Minor, opposite Cyprus. The victories were won in 1367 and 1361 respectively.

59. **the Grete See** The Mediterranean.

62. **Tramyssene** Now Tlemcen in Western Algeria.

65. **Palatye** Now Balat in Asia Minor, then ruled by a Seljuk Turk, later to be driven out by an Ottoman Turk.

70. **vileynye** Anything unbecoming a knight, or characteristic of a villein.

71. **no maner wight** No kind of person. **wight** Is in apposition to **maner**.

72. **verray** Not to be translated by *very*. It is an adjective, meaning *true*.

74. **Hors** Is plural.
he Refers to the knight.
gay Finely dressed. He wore his armour, for he had come straight from his latest campaign.

76. The first foot has been suppressed in this line.

77. **viage** Journey, rather than voyage, which suggests nowadays a journey by sea.

79. **Squyer** Squire. The eldest son of a knight was a squire by birth. After a severe training in courtly manners in a noble household, he would become an attendant on his master during a campaign, in order to complete his probation. The accomplishments attributed to this squire were those in which he had had instruction from his master and mistress. Chaucer had been a squire in the household of Lionel, Duke of Clarence. He had also at the age of twenty been on a campaign in Flanders.

80. **Bacheler** A candidate or probationer for knighthood.

84. And wonderly delyver(e) ‖ and of greet strengthe.

85. **chivachye** A mounted raid by knights and their retainers. As the Hundred Years' War was being fought in a desultory way at this time, these three northern provinces of France were always open to attack from Calais. This is Chaucer's only direct reference to the Hundred Years' War.

87. **As ... space** Considering his short period of service.

88. **his lady grace** His lady's favour. Certain feminine nouns in Old English showed no inflection for the genitive case. Compare 'Lord's Day' with 'Lady Day'.

89. The Squire was dressed fashionably in a short coat with very wide, long sleeves. Chaucer pokes fun at the extravagant embroidery on his coat; it looked like a meadow with its flowers.

94. **faire** Not fairly, but well.

95. **songes make** Compose the music.
endite Compose the words.

98. Mediaeval natural history taught that nightingales do not sleep in the mating season.

100. The duty of a squire included the carving of the joint in the presence of his master.

101. **Yeman** Yeoman. He was the Knight's servant, a small landowner, and possibly led a spare horse for him. His costume does not suggest that he had been with his master on the 'viage'.

102. **him liste** It pleased him. Do not say *he pleased*, for 'him' is dative with an impersonal verb.

103. His costume was that of a forester, as were also his accomplishments.

106. He could set his equipment in order as a yeoman should.

107. If the feathers were trimmed too closely, or if they were weak by nature, they would not allow the arrow to fly properly.

108. **a mighty bowe** Would be a good long-bow, like Robin Hood's.

112. The sword and buckler were also carried by Robin Hood for sport.

113. **that oother syde** Chaucer normally uses **that** for our 'the' with **other**.

115. **Cristofre** St Christopher was the patron saint of foresters.
shene Bright.

118. **Prioresse** She would be the head of a small religious house, with duties not unlike those of the headmistress of a high-class boarding school of today, for in addition to her religious duties, she was responsible for the education of a few ladies of the middle class, daughters of London citizens, perhaps.

119. **simple and coy** Modest and quietly charming, though not a coquette.

120. **Seint Loy** He brought Christianity to Flanders in the seventh century. It was the custom in the Middle Ages for even

churchmen to swear: the Prioress swore by a saint who was also an artist and of great personal beauty.

123. It has been suggested that certain parts of the service were sung through the nose to avoid straining the throat.

125. She spoke her French with an accent. The Convent of St Leonard at Stratford, where she had been educated, taught either the Norman or the Flemish dialect.

134. That in her coppe ‖ ther was no ferthing sene

137. **of greet disport** Merry.

143. She was so charitable ‖ and so pitous.

146. Nuns were forbidden by the Church to keep dogs: on the other hand, Court ladies did so. It may have been in an effort to imitate Court behaviour that she broke the law of the Church.

147. **wastel breed** The finest bread, made from white flour.

149. **men smoot it** This is the Middle English way of expressing a passive voice. 'If it were struck'.
Men Is used like the French *on*.

151. **wympel** This wrapper for the neck should have been of the plainest, and should have left exposed as much of the face as possible. The fact that the Prioress's was neatly pleated may have earned Chaucer's ironical and naïve praise: it indicated something of a well-bred lady's love for dainty things to wear.

152. **tretys** Well-formed.
greye as glas The usual expression for what we call 'blue eyes' (Manly).

154. **fair** Broad. It should have been covered by her wimple.

159. **peire** Set.
bedes Beads. Her rosary was a simple one, made of small coral, with every tenth bead, or gaud, in green. The gaud was for the 'Our Father', and the smaller ones for the 'Hail Mary'.

161. The 'A' stood for Latin *amor*, or Divine Love. The device shows the kingly might of Divine Love. 'Love conquers all things'.

164. The **chapeleyne** was her secretary. One of the three priests

was named Sir John; it was he who told the tale of the cock and the fox, perhaps the most charming of all the *Canterbury Tales*; the other two priests are nowhere else mentioned, and are not reckoned in the total of the pilgrims.

165. **a Monk** He was vowed to obedience and devotion, poverty and chastity, and included among his duties the supervision of the outlying estates of the convent to which he was attached. He was also the prior of a subordinate monastery, or 'cell' as it is called. He was a worldling, fond of hunting and feasting, and showed little interest in the religious life.

fair for the maistrye Fine, in an exceptional degree, a very fine specimen of a monk.

166. **outrydere** He had to ride about to supervise the *outlying* property of the monastery.

167. **a manly man** A fine figure of a man.

170. **gynglen** Infinitive mood, not a participle.

172. **ther as** Where.

173. **St Benedict** Founded the Benedictine Order of Monks to which this monk belonged.

St Maurus Was one of his early followers.

The rule Specified the vows required from each adherent to the Order.

174. The syntax of this line and the next seems at fault. Chaucer makes a violent change of construction after the end of line 174.

176. **the space** Meanwhile. Possibly **space** means *course*: the meaning would then be 'held his course according to the new fashion of the times'.

177. **text** Authority. The reference is to a passage in St. Jerome's works. A plucked hen would be of little value in Chaucer's time.

179. **recchelees** Careless of his vows.

183. Chaucer supports the Monk's attitude; or is his comment ironical?

184. **what** Why.

wood Mad, as sometimes in Shakespeare. Extra syllable is found before the cæsura.

186. **swynken** and **laboure** They have the same meaning. Notice that the former is of English origin and the latter of French.

187. **Austin** Is Augustine, not the monk who converted Kent to Christianity in 597, but the great Bishop of Hippo, the author of the *Confessions*, after whom the Augustinian friars took their name. His mother was St Monica.

189. **prikasour** One who tracked a hare by its footprints. Some give the word the meaning of a 'hard rider'.

190. **grehoundes** The first syllable of this word may signify 'swift'.

193. **sleves** A dissyllable.

194. **grys** A costly grey squirrel fur.
a lond Any land.

196. **curious** Elaborate, made with great care.

197. **love-knotte** An intricate knot, a symbol of true love.

200. **in good poynt** Is a literal translation of the French *en bon point*, stout. Scott's phrase in *Marmion* is 'in good case'.

201. **stepe** Bright, or prominent.

202. **stemed** Glowed.
leed Cauldron, made of lead.

203. **souple** Soft, pliant, another sign of luxury. The Wife of Bath also had 'soft' boots.

205. **forpyned** Tortured. The participle *for-* has an intensifying force.
goost Ghost has no *h*. Caxton introduced this letter from Flanders where he learned printing.

206. Monks were forbidden to eat meat.

207. **broun** Berries, as a rule, are red, and not brown; but in Old English 'brun' means bright, shining, as in *burnished*.

208. The friars were organized to live lives in the active service of their fellows, and supported themselves by begging. They were vowed to a life of poverty.
wantown Uncontrolled, carefree.

209. **limitour** One who was allowed to beg only within certain prescribed limits.
solempne Not 'solemn', but 'pompous', 'self-important'.

210. **ordres foure** There were four chief orders of friars, the Franciscans, the Dominicans, the Carmelites, and the Augustinians. They are also called the Grey, Black, White and Austin respectively. They were founded in the thirteenth century, and had between them about 170 convents in England.
can Knows.

211. **daliaunce** Gossip, small talk.
fair langage 'Pretty' language.

212. The marriages were conducted by the parish priest, or 'curat' as a rule, who would charge a fee. The hint given in line 208 of his character suggests that the young women mentioned may have been former concubines of his own.

214. An ironic statement.
noble post A noble pillar.

215. **biloved** Dissyllabic before cæsura.

216. **frankeleyns** Landowners of high standing, but ranking below barons; see lines 331–60.
contree The district in which he could beg.

217. **worthy** Of good position.
toun Village, neighbourhood.

220. **licenciat** The Friar had a licence from the authorities of his order to hear confessions and to grant absolutions. Those whose sins were such that the parish priest could not absolve them from penalty could have recourse to the Friar when *he* visited the community.

224. **ther as** In places where.
pitaunce Gift of food or money.

226. **y-shrive** Made a good confession and been absolved thoroughly.

227. **he yaf** i.e. the sinner.
he dorst i.e. the Friar.

230. **may** Can.

smerte It grieves him.

232. A gift to the Friar is a good sign of repentance.

237. **yeddynges** Ballads, tales, songs, probably including dances.

239. **champioun** Prize-wrestler, like Charles in *As You Like It*.

241. **tappestere** Barmaid. The word is feminine.

242. **lazar** Leper.

beggestere Beggar woman.

243. For unto a man of such an important position as his.

244. **as ... facultee** Considering his special duties.

247. The first syllable of the line has been suppressed.

251. **nas ... no ... nowher** These three negatives make a very strong negative. 'In no place at all was there anyone so capable.'

254. *In principio* These are the opening words of the Gospel according to St John, and were used by the friars in their visits, perhaps as a kind of charm with which to wheedle money from the ignorant poor.

255. **ferthyng** A bit, possibly a small coin.

256. **purchas** Money gained by his earnings, possibly fraudulently.

rent His income; but as he had no income, we must see a humorous application in the proverb. It is an understatement, suggesting that he got much money for his Order by his begging, though his methods would not bear investigation.

257. **rage** Frolic.

whelpe Puppy.

258. **love-dayes** These were days when disputes were settled without recourse to law.

259. **cloysterer** One of the poorer cloistered monks.

260. With a thredbare cope ‖ as is a poore scoler

261. **maister** A Master of Arts, who is here contrasted with the poor scholar, who had not yet gained his degree.

262. **semycope** Small cape.

263. That became as round as a bell as it was taken from the cupboard; or, perhaps, that became as round as a bell from the foundry, when the Friar put it on. The former meaning seems the more probable.

264. **wantownesse** Freak, whimsicality, affectation.

269. **worthy** Remarkable, excellent. Used ironically.

270 **marchant** He was engaged in the trade with Flanders of which we hear a great deal in connection with Edward III's reign. He seemed out to give a good impression of himself to the rest of the pilgrims. The forked beard was fashionable at this time, as can be seen from contemporary pictures.

271. **motteleye** This is not the motley of the court jester, but a 'rich cloth in which was woven a figured design, sometimes in the same colour as the ground, sometimes in another (Manly).
hye on horse This would help to give a distinction to his presence.

272. **Flaundrissh** Flemish. These beaver hats were expensive, as prices went then.

274. **resons** Opinions.
solempnely Pompously. We have all met people of this kind.

275. **sounynge** Proclaiming.
thencrees The increase.

276. **for any thing** At any cost. The North Sea was infested with pirates, against whom a merchant would certainly be bitter.

277. **Middelburgh** Near Flushing, and a staple for the wool trade.
Orewelle The port for Ipswich, on the river of that name.

278. **sheeldes** These were French gold coins bearing a shield, or *écu*, on one side of them. It was a royal prerogative to exchange coins, but this merchant had found a way of getting more than the current price in his exchangings.

280. This line may imply that he had no ready money.

281. So imposing was he in his management of his buying and selling and his transactions; but possibly **governaunce** means self-control.

282. **chevisaunce** Usury.

285. **Clerk** A 'Clerk in Holy Orders'. He had no doubt taken his B.A. and was continuing his studies for the Master's degree, with emphasis on logic (286) and philosophy (295).

286. **y-go** Gone, turned his attention.

290. **overest courtepy** Topmost short cape.

291. **benefice** A Church living.

292. **worldly** He was one who despised mundane things and so was hardly in the running when good jobs were going.
office Secular employment.

293. **hym was levere** It was more welcome to him.

294. **Twenty bookes** Before the introduction of printing, the expense of such a library would be great. It has been calculated that the sum he would like to spend on these volumes would buy three houses like those of London citizens. His poverty was due to his extravagance in buying books, although they were necessary for his study. Chaucer had 60 books, if we can believe a statement of his in his *Legend of Good Women*. The first syllable of the line is suppressed.

295. **Aristotle** A Greek philosopher.

297. Do not overlook Chaucer's sly thrust at the student of philosophy. The 'natural' philosopher was still trying to turn base metals into gold.

304. The garrulous Host rallied the Clerk on his shyness, in line 840.

305. Formally and respectfully. He must have felt very much out of his element in this particular pilgrimage.

306. **hy sentence** Deep meaning, elevated thoughts.

307. **sounynge in moral vertu** Tending to uplift his hearers.

308. He was at the same time a student at Oxford and a teacher.

309. **Sergeant of the Lawe** He would be a lawyer of high rank, who had had considerable practice of the law. From the small group of these sergeants, the judges of the Common Law were chosen. This Sergeant had acted as a temporary judge in

emergency, having a special commission from the king to act in this capacity.

war and wys Alert and prudent.

310. Scholars differ about the meaning of the term **parvys**. Some hold that it refers to the porch at St Paul's or Westminster Abbey where lawyers used to meet their clients for consultation; others say that it refers to the Court of the Exchequer which met at Westminster; still others say that it refers to meetings held for the instruction of young students in the Inns of Court. Whatever the correct meaning may be, it is clear that Chaucer intended to suggest the weight attached to the Sergeant's opinion and advice.

314. **assise** County courts.

315. **patente** Appointment to serve as judge.
commissioun Statement of the kind of cases he was to try. This Sergeant had a *full* commission: he could try all kinds of cases.

316. **science** Knowledge in general.

317. **robes** These were given to lawyers as part, or whole, payment of their fees; there is no suggestion of accepting rich robes as a bribe. There was not much money in circulation in Chaucer's days. See also the reference to the Merchant in l. 280.

318. **purchasour** Buyer-up of land.

319. **fee simple** The purchase and transfer of land is often a complicated process, involving many legal considerations. Fee-simple was the very simplest kind of tenure, for land so held was the absolute property of the seller, and so could be sold outright to the purchaser; but so skilled was the sergeant that the most complicated transaction seemed (to him) as easy as a case of 'fee-simple'.

320. **infect** Rendered of no effect, invalidated.

323. **termes** Legal phraseology.
caas Legal cases.
doomes Legal judgments.

325. **endite** Compose a charge in legal terms.
make a thing Draw up a deed in proper form (cf. l. 95).

326. **pinche** As Prof. Manly produces much evidence that Chaucer's Sergeant was by name Thomas Pynchbek, this word is a pun on the name.

328. **hoomly** Unostentatiously, quietly.

medlee This is cloth dyed before being woven; it was woven in stripes which were sometimes of different colours.

329. **barres** Ornamental bands.

331. **Frankeleyn** A wealthy landowner. Manly identifies him with Sir John Bussy who became Speaker of the House of Commons, and was executed for treason in 1399. He is Bushy in Shakespeare's *Richard II*. Chaucer wrote *The Frankeleyn's Tale*.

333. **complexioun** Temperament.

sangwyn Confident. The ancient doctors recognised four temperaments which characterized individuals. These were based on the four 'humours' of which the blood was composed, namely *sanguine* which was characterized by blood, *phlegmatic* by phlegm, *bilious* by bile, and *melancholic* by black bile. The blending of the four humours produced the complication or *complexion*, which we call temperament, though we no longer consider the physical basis of temperament to be what the mediæval doctors believed. See note to 411.

336. **Epicurus** He was a Greek philosopher who taught that the highest bliss for man was to have his *body* free from pain, and his *mind* from fears. This doctrine was distorted into one that taught that pleasure was the true end in life.

340. **St Julian** Was the patron saint of the hospitable.

341. **after oon** After one standard – and that a high one.

342. **bettre envyned** With a better wine-cellar.

343. **bakemete** Fish and meat pies, pasties. Only the rich could afford either fish or meat.

348. **mete** Food, especially dinner. He varied his diet according to the various seasons of the year.

349. **mewe** Coop for fattening fowls.

350. **stewe** Stew-pond, in which were kept live fish for fast days.

351. 'There was trouble for his cook.'

352. **poynaunt** Highly spiced.
gere Utensils.

353. **table dormant** Permanent table, as distinct from the trestle table which was set up for each meal as required. The Franklin's hospitality is shown by his having this fixed table always ready for chance comers.

355. **lord and sire** President, chairman.

356. **knight of the shire** Member of Parliament for the county.

359. **countour** Pleader in court; or, possibly, accountant (Manly).

360. **vavasour** Vassal's vassal. A franklin was not, however, a sub-vassal. It has been thought that the word may indicate a squire.

363. The livery must have been that of a religious brotherhood, for five men of different occupations would normally have five different liveries. These guilds are mentioned in connection with the Parson (511).
solempne Important.

367. An indication that the guildsmen were wealthy.

371. Scan: Éverich for the . . .

372. The **alderman** was the head of a guild.

376. A gibe at the social pretensions of women: see also the Prioress's aping of court manners, lines 151–62.

377. **vigilies** Meeting held on the evening before a guild festival.

378. **roialliche** Like a queen.

379. The **Cook** probably belonged to the guildsmen, not to the pilgrims as a body.
for the nones The phrase means originally 'for the occasion', but it developed a variety of meanings. Here it seems to mean 'fit, or suitable for the occasion'. As all the inns were not so well provided as the Tabard was, the engagement of the Cook was a wise precaution.

381. **poudre-marchant** Sour-tasting flavouring powder.
tart Bitter; no reference to pastry.

galingale A spiced root, possibly like ginger.

382. **London ale** Was superior to what they might find in the alehouses by the way.

384. **mortreux** A stew, made of meat or fish. (The first syllable of the line has been suppressed.)

386. **mormal** A cancerous sore.

387. **for** As for.
blankmanger Minced chicken, stewed with such ingredients as milk, eggs, rice, almonds and sugar.

388. **Shipman** He would be the captain of a trading vessel plying between Bordeaux and Dartmouth, which was then a considerable port. One Peter Risshenden of Dartmouth was master of a ship named 'The Maudeleyne' at this time.

390. **rouncy** A carthorse, or at least a strong horse.
as he couthe As well as he could, for sailors are awkward horsemen.

391. **faldyng** Was coarse cloth of serge.

395. **a good felawe** Often a euphemism for a rascal, as the following lines indicate in this instance.

397. **from Burdeaux-ward** On the journey from Bordeaux.
Chapman Merchant.

398. He took no account of finicky scruples of conscience.

400. He made them walk the plank. There were frequent complaints at this time of piracy on the high seas committed by men from Dartmouth.

401. As to his skill in reckoning his tides well.

402. **him bisydes** All round him.

403. **herberwe** Conditions of water in the harbours he frequented.
moone Phases of the moon.
lodemenage Skill as a pilot.

404. **Carthage** Probably Cartagena, on the east coast of Spain.

405. Prudent in his undertakings.

407. **as they were** In order.

408. **Gootland** Gotland, an island in the Baltic.
Cape Finisterre Is in North-West Spain.

409. **Bretayne** Brittany.

411. It will not be easy to understand the references in
connection with this Doctor of Medicine unless we have some
idea of the beliefs which governed medical practice at the time.
They were both 'scientific' and astrological. Under the first
heading we must realize that the doctors of the time were taught
that bodily health depended upon the equilibrium of four
factors, called 'humours'. These were fluids, known as
melancholy, phlegm, blood and bile of which the last three
certainly exist. When these were mixed in the right proportions
the patient was well; but when any irregularity occurred, the
bodily health was thrown out of gear, and illness resulted.
Moreover, the humours were characterized as possessing the
usual qualities of matter: melancholy was cold and dry; phlegm,
cold and moist; blood, hot and moist; and bile, hot and dry. The
combining of the humours was called 'complexion', and
controlled a person's temperament. The treatment of a malady
consisted of bleeding if the blood were in excess, and of purging
if the fault was in the other humours.

   But the Arabs taught that the various signs of the Zodiac ruled
definite parts of the body, and a careful doctor would not fail to
take account of the constellation controlling that part of the
body which he was attempting to treat. Treatment under this
heading consisted in making charms, 'images' they are called in
line 418, which were representations of the signs by which the
astrologers knew the various 'signs' of the Zodiac. These
talismans were thought to influence for good the patient who
was being treated. The planets had the greatest influence over a
person's health if the image was made when it was just coming
above the eastern horizon, in the 'ascendant', as the phrase
went.

413. **to speke of** With regard to.

414. **astronomye** We call it astrology.

415. **kepte** Watched over carefully.

416. **houres** Times of maximum planetary influence.

magik natureel Use of the forces of the universe as revealed by the study of astrology.

417. **fortunen the ascendent** Select a fortunate astrological moment for making the images, or talismans, when the planet concerned was just appearing (411).

420. See note on 411.

421. Where it had its origin.

422. **verray** Fine, excellent.

426. **letuaries** Medicinal preparations, mixed with honey.

429. The doctors mentioned in this list were the famous names in ancient and mediæval medicine. Esculapius was the founder of medicine, according to Greek mythology; Hippocrates was the greatest doctor of the Greek world. Galen was a Greek also, of the second century AD; Deiscorides and Rufus were his contemporaries. Avicen and Haly – Avicenna and Alhazen – were Persians, of the eleventh century; Razis, Serapion, Averrios, and Damascien were Arab doctors; while Constantius Afer was a Benedictine monk of the twelfth century. Gilbertyn was an English physician, as was Gatesden, who was physician to Edward II and the first Englishman to write about medicine. Bernard Gordon was a contemporary of Chaucer and Professor of Medicine at Montpellier.

438. An echo of the controversy between science and religion.

439. His clothing is an indication of his wealth.

440. Specially fine silks.

441. **esy of dispence** Not easy going, but moderate. In other words, he was a thrifty man, in spite of his fine clothes.

442. **pestilence** Is the plague, notably the Black Death of 1348–9. He would perhaps have served in the plagues of 1369 and 1376. Reference to contemporary events are very rare in Chaucer; see note to line 85.

443. **gold** Is a heart tonic in medicine; therefore he was particularly fond of gold. Notice the poet's sly dig at the Doctor's love of gold, and the possible 'explanation'.

445. **bisyde** Near. This woman had had five husbands, as line 460 tells us; from the Prologue to her tale we learn that she married first at 12 years old, and at the time of the pilgrimage she was anticipating the death of her fifth husband. Her Christian name was Alyson.

446. She lost her hearing as the result of a blow from her fourth husband, from whom she had snatched the 'book' he was reading about the wickedness of women.

447. The neighbourhood of Bath was noted for the manufacture of cloth. West of England cloth is still sought after.

448. **Ypres and Gaunt** Or Ghent, were very well reputed for their cloth weaving.

450. **the offrynge** The offertory was sung during the service of the mass, as men and women went up to the sanctuary to present their gifts of bread and wine. The procession was arranged in accordance with rank, and the Wife of Bath, being rich, had first place among the women.

454. A humorous exaggeration, though the structures women wore were often enormous.

458. **fair** Comely, not fair in the sense of blonde.

460. Formerly the weddings took place outside the church, and Mass was afterwards celebrated at the altar.

463. **Jerusalem** This word has three syllables: Jer'salem.

465. The list of the sacred places she visited includes many of the most notable shrines in Europe.
Rome Was the holy and eternal city.
Boulogne Contained a famous shrine of the Virgin.
Santiago In Galicia, contained the noted shrine of St James of Compostella.
Cologne Was said to hold relics of the three magi.

467. **Wandrynge by the weye** Possibly detours from the prescribed route for the pilgrims.

468. **gat-tothed** This word has given much trouble to commentators. It seems to mean either that her teeth were set

wide apart, i.e. gate-toothed; or that they were like goat's teeth, which project.

472. **foot-mantel** The drawing of her in one of the MSS shows an outer petticoat, evidently to protect her skirt.

473. She must have ridden astride.

475. **remedyes of love** Charms to secure the love of another, or to cure one's hopeless love.

476. **the olde daunce** This means she knew her subject from A to Z.

478. **Persoun** Rector. His poverty may have been due to his humble origin; his brother was a working-farmer.

486. **cursen** Excommunicate for non-payment of tithes.

489. **offryng** The Easter offering which was devoted to the rector himself.

his substaunce Was his private property, which must have been scanty.

491. **parisshe** Is trisyllabic.

494. **muche and lyte** Rich and poor.

498. The reference is to *St Matthew* v. 19.

499. **figure** Illustration

500. 'If the priest in whom we trust be sinful, what wonder is it that an uneducated man should show signs of corruption?'

507. The absentee priest was one of the scandals of the time. Some clergy would forsake their parishes, and, leaving the district in charge of a hired priest, would seek for themselves the easier post of saying masses for the dead, in a chantry chapel. Other priests would get appointments as chaplains to a guild.

513. There are several references in this section to *St John's Gospel*, Chapter x.

514. **mercenarie** Hireling.

515. He himself was virtuous.

516. **despitous** Scornful.

517. **daungerous** Domineering. The word 'daunger' may derive from Latin *dominus*.

digne Disdainful.

520. **ensample** The final -*e* is syllabic before the cæsura.

521. **but it were** But were there. 'It' often plays the part in Middle English now taken by 'there', e.g. 'it was a king' stands for 'there was a king'.

522. **what so** Who ever he was.

523. **for the nonys** The phrase seems meaningless here, and is possibly used to provide a rhyme for **noon is**.

526. **spiced conscience** An unbending conscience.

527. This line illustrates a quaint piece of Middle English syntax. We must translate by 'the teaching of Christ and His twelve Apostles . . .'

529. **A Plowman** Was not a serf: he may indeed have been the holder of a small farm under the Church.

534. An impersonal construction: it profited him or cost him dear, caused him joy, or sorrow.

540. **propre** Own.
catel Property, or perhaps, cattle. Probably the line means 'Both of his own work and his cattle's'.

541. It was a sign of his poverty that he rode on a mare; the other pilgrims had horses.
tabard Smock.

545. The miller, owning the only mill in a village, could charge what he liked for grinding corn.

547. **proved wel** Stood him in good stead.
overal ther Wherever.

548. **the ram** The usual prize at a wrestling match.

549. **short-sholdered** i.e. his upper arms were short.

554. **cop right** The very top.

560. **goliardeys** Foul-mouthed buffoon.

561. **harlotryes** Disreputable tales.

562. **tollen** Take the toll a miller was entitled to in return for grinding his neighbours' corn.

563. **thombe of gold** There is a proverb that an honest miller has a thumb of gold, but its meaning is ambiguous. It may mean that as a golden thumb is unheard of, so is an honest miller. On the other hand, it may mean that as his thumb was used to test the quality of the corn he had to grind, it was through his thumb that he made his wealth.

566. The Miller led the procession from the Tabard, while the Reeve brought up the rear (l. 622).

567. **Manciple** He was a housekeeper for a company of lawyers. As a class they seem to have been characterized by sharp practices, as was this specimen.

a temple These precincts were the homes of lawyers, who had succeeded to the property once owned by the Knights Templars, on the south side of the Strand. '**a**' means *one of the* temples.

568. **achatour** Caterer.

570. **taille** Tally. Formerly those who bought on credit received a strip of wood, notched in accordance with the amount of the purchase. The seller had a similar record of the amount. When the account was settled, the tallies were burnt.

577. **curious** Skilful.

581. **by his propre good** On his own income.

582. **but-if** Unless.

585. **caas** Legal case, though the word may be singular or plural.

586. **sette hir aller cap** Made fools of them all. That is, he cheated them without being found out.

hir aller An example of an old genitive case, meaning 'of them all'.

587. **Reve** He was the manager of the estate, and superior to the other servants, as line 603 suggests. Notice how carefully Chaucer describes his personal appearance.

594. **auditour** He was sent by the lord to check the accounts kept by the Reve; but no auditor could get the better of Oswald of Baldeswelle, in Norfolk.

595. According to whether it had been a dry or a wet season.

601. **yeer** This form is both singular and plural. We still talk of a two-year old, using the singular form of year.

603. **bailliff** He managed more estates than one, and so was superior to the Reeve; but the latter knew all his peccadilloes.

604. Whose cunning and trickery he did not know.

605. **deeth** The plague.

608. He could make purchases more advantageously than his lord could.

611. **to yeve** By giving and lending him of the lord's own property.

617. **surcote** Outer coat.
pers Blue-grey cloth.

620. **Baldeswelle** Is near Dereham, in Norfolk.

621. His long coat was tucked into his girdle, like that of the famous Friar Tuck.

622. We gather from the later parts of the *Canterbury Tales* that the Miller and the Reve were ill friends. They put the whole length of the procession of pilgrims between them at the beginning.

623. **Somnour** The Summoner was attached to an ecclesiastical court as a server of writs-to-appear.

624. **cherubinnes** The cherubs in the paintings in churches were distinguished from seraphs by being coloured red, while the latter were blue.

625. **sawcefleem** Covered with white pimples, one symptom of leprosy, which was still common in England. His eyes were **narwe**, as a result of swollen eyelids. The words may perhaps be translated 'heavy with drink'.

626. **hoot** Hot, violent in conduct.
lecherous Lustful.

627. **scalled** Scurfy.
piled Scanty, as a result of his disease.

629. These were the customary remedies for leprosy.
quiksilver Mercury.
litarge Ointment made from lead oxide.

brimstoon Sulphur.
boras Borax.
ceruce White lead ointment.
oille of tarte Cream of tartar.

631. Cleanse and cauterize.

632. **helpen of** Cure him of.
whelkes Pimples.

633. **knobbes** Pustules.

634. These vegetables were almost the only ones eaten in England in the Middle Ages.

639. **termes** Legal phrases.

643. **Watte** Wat, or Walter, as in Wat Tyler.

644. But if anyone tested his knowledge in any other detail.

646. *Questio quid juris* The question is, what section of the law applies.

647. **harlot** Rascal.

648. **bettre felawe** Bigger rascal.

650. **good felawe** A euphemism for a rogue (see note to line 212). He would turn a blind eye on a friend's immorality.

652. **pull a finch** Plunder a fool, pluck a pigeon.

655. The Archdeacon would actually pass the sentence of excommunication.

656. **but-if** Unless. As the Archdeacon's punishment would be a fine, it was only the miser who would dread the sentence.

659–61. Chaucer appears as the orthodox churchman, defending the regular teaching of the Church.

661–2. Notice the rhyme.

662. *Significavit* This was the first word in the writ authorizing the seizure of the goods of an excommunicated person.

663. **daunger** Complete control.
at his owne gyse In his own way.

664. **girles** Young people of both sexes: the meaning was not confined to young females till the sixteenth century.

665. **al** Entirely, in everything.

667. **alestake** A bush suspended over the entrance indicated that ale could be bought where the sign was found.

668. Possibly indications that he was drunk.

669. **Pardoner** A seller of pardons the purchase of which remitted a portion of a penance imposed.

670. **Rouncival** A 'cell' of the Priory of Our Lady of Roncesvalles, in the Pyrenees, had been established at Charing Cross. Any friend and comrade of the Summoner would hardly be respectable. The modern hospital is a relic of the foundation.

671. **Rome** The word is a dissyllable. At the time at which Chaucer wrote, there were rival Popes, at Rome and at Avignon (1378–1417). England sided with the Pope at Rome.

672. This must be some part of a 'popular song' of the time.

673. A strong droning base.

680. **for jolitee** For pleasure, he was enjoying the pilgrimage.

682. **the newe jet** The latest fashion.

683. **dischevele** With hair untidy.

685. **Vernicle** St Veronica, according to legend, lent her handkerchief to Christ to wipe His face as He carried His cross to Calvary. When He returned it, it bore the imprint of His face. A vernicle was a copy of this portrait.

687. This line suggests Chaucer's attitude to the question of pardons.

688. His goat's voice must have been drowned by the Summoner's bourdon.

692. **Berwyk unto Ware** From one end of England to the other.

695. **Oure Lady veyl** There was no genitive inflexion to the word 'Lady' in Old English.

699. **latoun** A kind of brass. The 'stones' would be semi-precious, used as an ornament of the cross.

702. **person** parson. The two words were originally pronounced alike, the *er* being sounded *ar*, as in modern 'clerk'.

up on lond Up country, in a remote part.

703. **him** For himself, i.e. the Pardoner.

705. **japes** Tricks, foolish tales.

706. **made ... his apes** Made fools of them.
apes Dupes.

707. **atte laste** To sum up.

708. **ecclesiaste** Preacher.

709. **lessoun** A passage from the Scriptures or from the writings of the Church Fathers.
storie The legend of a saint.

710. **offertorie** During the service of the mass, the people presented their offerings, formerly of bread and wine, but later of money. The Pardoner sang during the collection, which was for the benefit of the church.
alderbest Best of all. *Alder* is for O.E. *calra*, genitive plural of *eall*, meaning *all*. See also line 823, where the form is *aller*.

712. **affyle** Smooth, put an edge on, make smooth.

715. **shortly** In brief.
in a clause In a few words.

716. **tharray** The array, attire.

718. **gentil** Excellent.

721. **how that we baren us** How we occupied our time; what we did.

722. As in Modern French, the verb of motion required the verb 'to be' as its auxiliary. Hence, **were alight**.

723. **viage** Journey, not necessarily by sea. The modern form 'voyage' has been borrowed in recent times from French, and is not directly derived from **viage**.

726. **narette** Ne + arette. The negative has become part of the main verb.

727. **pleynly** Openly, fearlessly, without regard to feelings of delicacy.

728. **to telle** In telling.

729. **properly** Characteristically of the speaker. Chaucer apologizes for repeating the coarse words of the ribald characters, like the Summoner, or even the Wife of Bath.

732. **reherce** Repeat.

734. **large** Freely, without restraint, broadly.

737. **althogh he were** Even if it were his brother's word he was repeating.

739. **brode** Unreservedly.

740. **vileynye** Ill-breeding.

741. **whoso that can him rede** If anyone can read him. Plato's works had been translated into Latin by Augustine, and other Church Fathers, but it was not till the Renaissance, a century after Chaucer's death, that Englishmen learnt to read the original Greek.

742. **cosyn** Nearly related to.

744. **in hir degree** According to their station in life. Orders of precedence were of very considerable importance then, even more than they are now.

746. Some of Chaucer's fun is seen here. His 'wit', or intelligence, was in no way 'short', for as a page in the household of Lionel, Duke of Clarence, he must have known much about the relative values of ranks. It has been suggested also that this line hints at Chaucer's amused contempt for the whole subject of the scale of values.

750. **us leste** It pleased us.

751. **our Hooste** His name was Harry Bailley, as we learn later on in the *Tales*. An innkeeper of this name, living in Southwark, was twice M.P. for the borough in the reigns of Edward III and Richard II.

752. **marchal in an halle** He would require a knowledge of precedence, such as Chaucer disclaimed for himself. He would be a kind of Master of Ceremonies.

754. **in Chepe** Cheapside was then London's market place, and a study of the names of streets branching from it right and left

will suggest what wares were sold in particular parts of the market. We find Bread Street, Milk Street, Wood Street, etc. As the citizens lived over the shops where they acquired their wealth, it was a high compliment to Harry Bailley to say that no finer citizen than he lived in the great London city itself.

760. Like a prudent man, the Host required settlement of bills before he began to make merry with his guests.

762. **lordynges** Sirs, gentlemen, my masters.

763. **by my trouthe, if that I shal not lye** A humorous form of asseveration.

766. **doon yow myrthe** Make you merry, make fun for you.

767. **myrthe** Bit fun.

775. **maken yow disport** Make fun for you.

776. **confort** Something cheerful to beguile the weariness of the journey.

780. **weye** Road. The Pilgrims' way from London to Canterbury led via Old Kent Road, Deptford, Blackheath, Welling, Dartford, Rochester, Sittingbourne and Ospringe. Pilgrims coming from the south country would avoid London and use the so-called 'Pilgrims' Way' through Surrey.

781. **my fader soule that is deed** A Middle English peculiarity of syntax. We should say: 'By the soul of my father who is dead'. Notice that **fader** bears no sign of the genitive case. In older English the words expressing relationships had uninflected genitives.

782. The cæsura follows **mery**.

784. We were not long in making up our mind.
conseil Resolution, decision.

785. **make it wys** Making it a subject of serious discussion.

787. **seye his verdit** Announce his decision.

788. **for the beste**: With your best attention.

789. **taak it ... in desdeyn** Despise it, make fun of it.

791. **to shorte with your weye** To shorten your way with, to beguile the time.

792. Chaucer tells us in line 24 that there were twenty-nine pilgrims, including himself. With the addition of the Host, and the Canon's Yeoman who joined the others on the way there would be 31 altogether. Four times 31 is 124; this was the great number of stories the author would require to get together to complete his scheme. It can hardly be wondered that the *Canterbury Tales* is a fragment only.

795. **whilom** Once upon a time.

797. **in this case** On this occasion.

798. Highest moral teaching and edification.

799. **our aller cost** The cost of us all. 'Our aller' is a survival of the Old English 'Ure ealra', a genitive plural.

800. **sittynge by this post** A dramatic touch; we can imagine the Host's slapping the post as he spoke, to emphasize his point.

810. **swore** This must be a past participle. The promise was made and our oaths were sworn.

813. **governour** Leader, controller.

814. **reportour** Critic, judge.

815. **certeyn** Fixed, definite. Our modern phrase, 'A certain price', is often quite indefinite: it may even be used to conceal what the actual price was.

817. **heigh and lowe** In all things.

823. **oure aller cok** See line 799, 'our aller cost'. The **cok** is supposed in folk-lore to believe that he rouses the sun.

826. **wateryng of Saint Thomas** This was a brook by the second milestone from London on the Old Kent Road, about half-an-hour's ride from the Tabard. Its site is between 509 and 511 Old Kent Raod, according to modern numberings.

827. **bigan his hors areste** Stopped his horse. 'Bigan to . . .' is to be translated by 'began to . . .', but **bigan** without **to** is an auxiliary verb for forming the past tense.

829. **I it yow recorde** I recall it to you; I remind you of it.

830. They may have changed their mind after 'sleeping on the idea' of the Host.

832. Another humorous asseveration.

838. The use of the plural form **draweth** indicates a polite form of address. Especially is this clear when he addresses the Prioress alone with the verb **cometh**.

839. **neer** This is a comparative, meaning 'nearer'. Its positive is **ny**.

841. **ne studieth noght** Don't be in a brown study. The Knight, the Prioress, and the Clerk are all persons of some position.
ley hond to Begin.

844. **aventure, or sort, or cas** Chance, luck, or fortune.

847. **resoun** Right (a noun), but we must say, 'as was only right'.

849. **what nedeth** Why is there need of.

851. **as he that wys was** Like one who was prudent.

853. **game** Amusement, entertainment.

Words which present special difficulties

The words in this list resemble closely words used in modern English, but they must be carefully distinguished from their apparent equivalents. Go over this list frequently, in order not to be caught out in a faulty piece of translation which might easily have been avoided by a thorough knowledge of vocabulary. Against each word is printed the number of the line where it first occurs in this text, and each word should be considered in its context.

herde 603

hoote 394

humour 421

infect 320

jet 682

juste 96

keep 398

large 734

late 77

lay 20

lenen 611

levere 293

licour 3

liveree 363

lusty 80

maistrye 165

male 694

may 230

men 149

mere 541

meschief 493

mete 127

mister 613

mote 232

neet 597

noon 210

offertorie 710

office 292

ounces 677

overal 216

paas 825

pace 36

pees 532

peire 159

pers 439

persoun 478

peyne 139

philosophre 297

piled 627

pinche 151

pitaunce 224

pleyn 315

port 69

poynaunt 352

poynt 200

presse 81

prikyng 191

propre 540

prys 67

purchas 256

quik 306

quyte 770

rage 257

reed 665

reede 90

sentence 306

shapen 772

shaply 372

sheeldes 278

shene 115

shortly 30

solaas 798

solempne 209

somtyme 65

song 122

sonne 7

soote 1

sort 844

sounynge 275

sovereyn 67

space 35

stemed 202

stepe 201

stewe 350

streite 457

strike 676

taille 570

tappestere 241

tart 381

terme 323

text 177

thanne 12

therto 48

thing 325

thinketh 37

tho 498

thoughte 385

til 180

trouthe 46

twinne 835

verray 72

vileynye 70

waited 525

wan 442

wantown 208

war 157

webbe 362

werre 47

what 184

whelke 632

whiche 40

whit 238

wonder 483

wood 184

worthy 43

wyf 445

wys 68

ye 10

yeddynges 237

y-go 286

Glossary

Note: Chaucer uses *i* and *y* as equivalents; *ou* and *ow* are interchangeable; as are *-ey-* and *-ay-* (which may also be written *-ei-* or *-ai-*).

The student is advised to consult the Textual notes in association with this Glossary.

a *any*, 194; *one*, 703
a *in, on*
able *fit*, 167; *capable*, 584
aboven *above*
absolutcioun *absolution*
accord *contract, decision*
accordant *in accordance with*
accorde *agree*, 830; **acorded** *agreed*, 818; *suited*, 244
achaat *purchasing*
achatour *buyer of provisions, caterer*
adoun *down*
adrad *frightened*
adversitee *adversity*
aferd *afraid*
affyle *soften, polish, make smooth*
after *afterwards*, 162; *according to*, 125
agayn *back again*, 801; *against*, 66
al *all; entirely, quite*, 248; *although*, 734
al be that *although*
alderbest *best of all*
alderman *head of a guild*
ale-stake *see note to l. 667*
algate *always*
alight *descended from horseback*
aller *see* **al**
als *as*
almoost *almost*
al-so *in addition*, 64; *as*, 730
alwey *always, continually*

amblere *an ambling horse*
amonges *amongst*
amorwe *on the next day*
amyable *pleasant, amiable*
anlaas *two-edged hunting knife, dagger*
anon *at once*
anoon *see* **anon**
anoynt *anointed*
ape *dupe*
apothecarie *preparer of drugs, or medicines*
apyked *trimmed*
aqueyntaunce *acquaintance*
arreste *stop*
arette *attribute to*
aright *wholly*, 189; **aright as**, *just as*, 267
armee *armed expedition*
array *array, dress, equipment*
arrerage *arrears*
arwe *arrow*
aryse *accrue, arise*
ascendent *the degree of the imaginary celestial circle of the sun's orbit which is above the horizon at a given moment. See note to l. 417*
asonder *scattered*
assent *consent*
assente *consent, agree to*
assoilyng *absolution*
astored *stocked*

astronomye *astrology*
atte *at the*
avaunce *profit*
avaunt *boast*
aventure *luck, chance, accident*
avys *deliberation*
awe *dread, fear*
ay *always*
baar see **bere**
bacheler *a candidate for knighthood*
bad see **bidden**
baggepipe *bagpipe*
baillif *bailiff*
bake *bake*
bakemete *pies, pastries*
balled *bald*
bar see **bere**
bare *uncovered, bareheaded*
bargayne *bargain*
barge *ship*
barre *ornamental bands*
bataille *battle*
bathed *bathed*
bawdrik *baldric, a belt worn across the chest*
bedde *bed*
bede *bead of a rosary*
been *to be*
beggere *beggar man*
beggestere *beggar woman*
ben see **been**
benefice *a cure of souls, a living*
benygne *kindly*
berd *beard*
bere *bear, conduct*
berye *berry*
bet *better*
beth see **been**
bettre *better*
bevere *made of the fur of the beaver*
bidden *to command*
bifalle *to happen*
bifore *before, 450; in front of, 377*
biforn *before, in front, 590; in the presence of, 100*

bigan biganne bigynne *to begin*
biloved *beloved*
bisette *employ*
bisily *earnestly*
business *business, anxiety, attention*
bismotered *soiled*
bisy *busy;* **bisier** *busier*
bisyde *near*
bit see **bidden**
bitwixe *between*
blade *sword*
blak *black*
blame *to be blamed*
blankmanger see note to l. 387
blede *to bleed*
blew *blue*
blisful *blessed*
blithe *happy, glad*
boille *boil*
bokeler *buckler, small shield*
boold *fearless, bold*
boote *remedy*
bootes *boots*
boras *borax*
bord *table, for meals*
born see **bere**
bowe *longbow*
bracer *guard for the wrist, used in archery*
bras *brass*
brawn *muscle*
breed *bread*
breem *bream, a fresh-water fish*
breeth *breath*
breken *smash, break to pieces*
brest *breast*
bretful *brimful*
bretherhed *brotherhood, guild, fraternity*
brimstoon *brimstone, sulphur*
brode *plainly, without reserve*
brooche *brooch*
brood *broad, wide*
broun *brown, burnished, shining*
brydel *bridle*

burdoun *accompaniment in the base,* *a drone*

burgeys *citizen, burgess*

but-if *unless*

by *on*

by-cause *because*

bynne *bin, for storing corn*

byte *cauterize*

byyinge *purchasing*

caas *accident, case,* 545; *legal cases,* 323

cacchen *catch*

cake *flat loaf of bread, cake*

calf *calf of the leg*

cam see **comen**

can see **connen**

cappe *cap*

carf see **kerven**

carl *fellow*

carpe *chatter*

cas see **caas**

catel *property, possessions*

ceint *girdle*

celle *monastery dependent on a larger* *house*

certeinly *certainly*

certyn *certainly,* 375; *fixed, definite,* 815

ceruce *white lead*

chambre *room*

champioun *prize-fighter*

chaped *mounted, capped*

chapeleyne *female chaplain,* *secretary*

chapman *merchant, trader*

charge *undertaking, responsibility*

charitable *sympathetic*

charitee *christian love*

chaunged *changed, varied*

chaunterie *chantry, fees for singing* *mass*

chekes *cheeks*

chere *manner,* 139; *face,* 857, *entertainment,* 747

cherubinnes *of a cherub*

chevisaunce *money lending*

chiere see **chere**

chiknes *chickens*

chirche *church*

chivachye *mounted expedition*

chivalrye *knightly conduct*

clad see **clothe**

clasp *buckle*

clause *sentence, a few words*

cleere *clearly*

clene *clean, pure*

clennesse *purity*

clense *purify, cleanse*

clepen *call*

clerk *student for Holy Orders, scholar*

cloke *cloak*

clooth *cloth*

clothe *clothe, bind, cover*

cloysterer *one who lives in a cloister,* *a monk*

cloystre *cloister*

cofre *chest, treasury*

cok *cock*

cold *cold*

colerik *choleric, quick-tempered*

colpon *shred, bundle, hank*

comen *to come*

commissioun *royal warrant*

companye *company, fellowship*

compeer *bosom friend, comrade*

complexioun *temperament*

composicioun *agreement*

concubyn *light o' love, mistress*

condicioun *state, rank in life,* *standing*

confort *pleasure, entertainment*

connen *to know*

conscience *tender-heartedness,* 112; *conscientiousness,* 398; *conscience,* 526

conseil *secret intention,* 665; *advice,* 784

contree *country, district*

cop *top*

cope *cape*

coppe *cup*

corage *heart, feeling, intent, disposition*

cordial *a heart stimulant, cordial*

cosyn *related to, akin to*

cote *coat*

coude see **connen**

countour *auditor.* See note l. 359

countrefete *imitate*

cours *course*

courtepy *short coat, cape*

couthe see **connen**

covenant *agreement*

coverchiefs *head coverings, kerchiefs*

cover *lay a table*

covyne *trickery, deceit*

coy *quiet, modest, shy*

craft *skill*, 401; *profession*, 692

crie *cry out, shout*

Christen *Christian*

Cristofre *a figure of St Christopher, worn as a charm.* See note l. 115

crop *new shoot*

crown *crown, surmount with a crown*

croys *cross*

crulle *curly, curled*

cryke *creek, inlet*

curat *parish priest*

cure *care, attention*

curious *carefully made, beautiful*, 196; *expert*, 577

curs *excommunication, curse*

cursen *curse, excommunicate*

cursyng *excommunication*

curtesye *courtly behaviour*, 46; *politeness*, 725

curteys *courteous, with courtly manners*, 99; *deferential*, 250

cut *lot, decisive choice*

daliaunce *gossip, small talk, familiar conversation*

dar dorste *to dare*

dauncen *dance*

daunce *dance*

daunger *risk*, 402; *control, jurisdiction*, 663

daungerous *domineering, haughty, hard to please, awkward*

dayerye *dairy*

dayesye *daisy*

decree *decree, document*

dede *deed;* **in dede** *indeed*

deed *dead*

deef *deaf*

deel *share, part;* **a greet deel** *largely, to a great extent*

deelen *concern oneself with, be friendly with*

deeth *death, especially the Black Death, plague*

degree *rank, station of life*

delve *dig*

delyt *delight, pleasure*

delyvere *active, sprightly, quick*

depe *deeply*

desdeyn *contempt, disdain*

despitous *scornful, contemptuous*

dette *debt*

detteless *free from debt*

devout *pious, devout*

devys *direction, decision*

devyse *relate, describe*

deyntee *rare, choice*, 168; *rarity, dainty*, 346

deys *dais, platform*

dide see **doon**

diete *diet, eating*

digne *worthy*, 141; *scornful*, 517

diligent *painstaking, hard-working*

diocise *diocese, district*

dischevelee *dishevelled, with hair unkempt*

discreet *tactful, discreet*

dispence *expenses, expenditure*

disport *cheerfulness, entertainment, diversion*

divyne *divine*

doctour *doctor, physician*

dokked *cut short, close cropped*

dong *dung, manure*

doom *judgment, legal decision*

doon dooth dide *do*
dore *door*
dormant *fixed, permanent.* See note
 l. 353
dorste see **dar**
doumb *dumb*
doute *doubt*
draughte *draught, drink*
drawen *draw,* 842; *lead,* 519
drede *dread, fear exceedingly*
dresse *prepare, set in order*
drogges *drugs, medicines*
droghte *drought*
drope *drop*
dronken see **drynken**
droupe *droop.* See note l. 107
drye *dry.* See note l. 420
drynken dronken *drink*
duzeyne *dozen*
dyere *dyer*
dyke *make ditches*
ecclesiaste *preacher*
ech *each, every*
echon *each one*
eek *also*
effect *reality*
elles *else, otherwise*
embrouded *adorned, embroidered*
encombre *encumber, hamper, stick
 fast*
encrees *increase*
endite *compose,* 95; *draw up in legal
 form,* 325
engendred *produced, generated*
ensample *example, pattern*
entuned *intoned*
envyned *supplied with wine*
er *before*
ercedeken *archdeacon*
ere *ear*
erly *early*
erst *before, at first*
eschaunge *exchange.* See note
 l. 278
ese *ease, entertainment, comfort*

esen *entertain, accommodate*
esily *at her ease*
estaat, estat *condition,* 203; *rank,*
 522
estatlich *stately*
esy *easy.* See note l. 441
even *moderate, average*
evermore *always*
everich *every, each*
everichon *every one*
everydeel *entirely*
exemple *example*
eye *eye*
facultee *profession, authority,
 position*
fader *father*
fair *excellent, very good,* 154; *a good
 one,* 165
faire *excellently, gratefully, neatly*
fairnesse *beauty of example,
 integrity, goodness*
faldyng *coarse cloth*
fallen falle fil fille *fall, occur,
 happen*
famulier *on friendly terms*
farsed *stuffed, crammed with*
faste *close, near*
fayn *gladly*
fee simple *unrestricted possession.*
 See note l. 319
feith *religion, faith*
felawe *companion, comrade.* See note
 l. 395
felawshipe *company*
felicitee *happiness*
fer ferre ferrer ferreste *far*
ferne *ancient, distant*
ferther *further*
ferthing *a trace,* 134; *a small gift,*
 255
festne *fasten*
fet *fetched*
fether *feather*
fetis *elegant, neat, graceful*
fewe *few*

feyne *pretend, feign, lie*
fiftene *fifteen*
fighten foughten *fight*
figure *figure of speech, illustration, simile*
fil see **fallen**
first, firste *first of all*, 161; *first,* 831
fithele *fiddle*
flessh *flesh meat*
flex *flax*
flour *flower*
flour-de-lys *lily-flower*
floytynge *playing the flute*
folwen folwed *follow*
fond see **fynden**
foo *foe, enemy*
foot-mantel see note l. 472
for *since, seeing that*
foreward *agreement, promise*
forheed *forehead*
forme *due form*
forneys *furnace*
forpyned *wasted by torture*
forster *forester*
fortunen *give good or bad fortune to.* See note l. 417
foryeve *forgive*
fother *cart-load*
foughten see **fighten**
foul *foul, impure*
fowel *bird*
frankeleyn *a freeholder.* See note l. 331
fraternitee *guild, brotherhood*
fredom *liberality, generosity*
freend *friend*
frere *friar*
fressh *bright fresh*
fro *from*
frye *fry*
ful *full,* 306; *very,* 22
fustian *coarse cloth*
fyn *fine*
fynch *finch.* See note l. 652

fynden fond *find*
fyr-reed *as red as fire*
gadrede *gathered*
gaf see **yeve**
galingale *the aromatic root of the sweet cypress*
game *jest,* 853; *please,* 534. See note
gan used to form past tense, with the sense of *did.* With participle *to* means *began*
garleek *garlic*
gat see **geten**
gat-tothed *with gaps between the teeth*
gauded *with large beads, known as gauds.* See note l. 159
gay *finely dressed,* 74; *handsome,* 111; *merry,* 296
geldyng *gelding*
gentil *of noble birth,* 72; *well disposed,* 567; *comfortable,* 718
gere *utensils,* 352; *clothing,* 365
gerland *garland*
gerner *granary*
gesse *suppose, think, imagine*
geten gat *obtain*
gilty *guilty, sinful*
gipser *pouch, bag*
girdel *girdle, belt*
girles *young people of both sexes*
girt *wearing a girdle*
glad *happy, glad*
gladly *gladly, readily*
glarynge *staring*
glas *glass, mirror*
gobet *piece, fragment*
goliardys *a buffoon, foul-mouthed jester*
gonne see **gan**
good *good,* 183; *goods, property,* 581
goon *go go*
goost *ghost*
goot *goat*
gospel *gospel*

governaunce *control, management*
governour *umpire, governor, controller*
governyng *control, management*
gowne *gown*
grace *favour*
graunten *agree to*
grece *grease*
greet gretter greteste *great*, 84; *a great one*, 339
grehoundes *greyhounds*
grene *green*
greye *bright*
greyn *grain*
grope *test, search deeply*
ground *texture*, 453; *instruct*, 414
grys *gray fur, possibly of squirrel*
gyde *guide, leader*
gynglen *jingle*
gypoun *tunic, short vest*
gyse *fashion*
haberdassher *a dealer in small wares, haberdasher*
habergeoun *a coat of mail, habergeon, hauberk*
halfe *half*
halle *hall, living room*
halwe *shrine, saint*
han see **haven**
hangen heng heeng henge *to hang*
happe *happen, befall*
hardily *boldly, certainly, surely*
hardy *bold, courageous*
hare *hare*
harlot *fellow, rascal*
harlotrye *unseemly jests, scurrilous tales*
harm *matter for regret, pity*
harneysed *mounted, ornamented*
harpyng *playing on the harp*
harre *hinge, hinges*
haten highte *to be called*
haunt *practice, skill, habit*

haven hath han hadde hade *have*
haven *harbour*
heed *head*
heede *heed, care, attention*
heeld see **holden**
heeng see **hangen**
heep *crowd, number*
heer heres *hair*
heeth *heath*
heere herde herd *hear*
heigh *high*, 316. See also note l. 817
helle *hell*
helpen *to help*, 258; **helpen of**, *cure*, 632; **holpen**, 18
hem *them*
heng see **hangen**
henten *seize, catch*
herberwe *harbour*, 403; *inn*, 765
herde *shepherd, herdsman*
herde see **heere**
here see **heer**
herknen herkneth *listen*
herte *heart*
herys see **heer**
hertely *cordially, sincerely*
hethen *heathen*
hethenesse *heathendom*
heven *heaven*, 519; *heave, lift*, 550
hewe *complexion, colour*
hider *hither*
highte see **haten**
him *him*
himself *himself*
himselven see **himself**
hipe *hip*
hir *their*
hir *her*
his *his*
holden heeld hoold *consider, keep, hold*
holpen see **helpen**
holt *wood, copse*
holwe *hollow, empty*

homward *on the way home*
hond *hand*
honest *honourable, respectable*
honour *honourable conduct*
hood *hood*
hoole *whole*
hoolly *completely, wholly*
hooly *holy*
hoom *home*
hoomly *in a plain, homely manner*
hoost *inn-keeper, host*
hoote *hot, fervent*, 394; *hotly, fervently, ardently*, 97
hors *horse, horses*
hosen *stockings*
hostelrye *inn, hostelry*
hostiler *inn-keeper*
hound *hound, dog*
houre *an astrological hour.* See note l. 416
house *convent, monastery*, 252; *house, mansion*, 343
housbond *husband*
housholdere *head of a household*
humour *humour.* See note l. 421
hy hyer *high, lofty*
hye *high, aloft*
hyndreste *hindmost, last*
hyne *farm-servant*
hyre *hire, rent*
i-drawe see **drawen**
ilke *same*
infect *invalidated, proved illegal*
inne *in*
inspire *to animate, quicken*
iren *iron*
janglere *noisy fellow, loud talker*
jape *jest, trick*
jay *jay, a bird*
jet *fashion, style*
jolitee *bravado, fun*
juge *judge, umpire*
juggement *opinion, decision*
justen *joust, tilt in the lists*
justice *judge*

keep *heed, care, attention*
kene *keen, sharp*
kepe kepte *keep, take heed*, 130, 512; *take care of*, 415; *guarded*, 276
kepere *keeper, prior*
kerven carf *carve*
knarre *thick-set fellow*
knobbe *boil, knob*
knowen knew *know*
knyf *knife*
kynde *kindly*
laas *cord, lace, string*
labouren *toil*
lady *lady.* See note to l. 88
lafte see **leven**
lakken *be lacking to*
langage *language, words*
lappe *lap*
large *large, broad*, 472; *freely*, 734
late *recently*
latoun *latten.* See note l. 699
lay see **liggen**
lazar *leper*
lecherous *lustful, wanton*
leed *leaden cauldron*
leef levere *pleasant, welcome*
leene *lean, thin*
legge *leg*
lekes *leeks*
lenen *lend*
lenger see **long**
length *height, length*
lernen lerned *learn*
lernynge *instruction*
lessoun *lesson as read in church.* See note l. 709
lest *pleasure, desire, delight*
leste see **listen**
leten leet lat *let, allow, permit, abandon;* **lat be** *put aside*, 840; **lat se** *let us see*, 831
letuaries *remedies, powders mixed with honey*
leven lafte *cease*

levere see **leef**

lewed *ignorant of book learning, uneducated*

leyen leyd *lay, place*

licentiat *a friar holding a licence from the pope to hear confessions, licentiate*

licour *sap*

liggen lay *lie, lodge*

liketh *it pleases you*

liknen *resemble*

limitour *limitor.* See note l. 209

lippe *lipe*

lipsen *lisp*

listen liste leste *it pleases*

listes *the lists at a tournament*

litarge *litharge, ointment made from lead oxide*

lite *little, small*

litel *little*

liven livynge *live*

liveree *livery of a guild, uniform, habit*

lodemenage *steersmanship, skill as a pilot*

logik *logic*

lokkes *locks, curls*

long *land.* **upon lond** *in the country.*

long lenger *long*

longen *desire greatly, yearn*

looken *look, seem*

looth *unwilling, reluctant*

lord *master*

lordynges *sirs, my masters*

lore *teaching, doctrine, learning*

loude *loudly*

love *love,* 475; *sweetheart,* 672

lovedays *lovedays.* See note l. 258

loveknotte *love-knot*

lovyere *lover*

lowe *low.* See note l. 107

lowly *humble*

luce *pike*

lust *delight, pleasure*

lusty *merry, joyful, gay*

lye *tell falsehoods, lie*

lyf *life*

lyk *like*

lynen *to line*

lyte *little*

lyve *life*

maad see **maken**

madame *my lady, madame*

made see **maken**

magik *magic.* See note l. 416

maister maistre *master, one in authority*

maistrye *superiority, excellence, authority.* See note l. 165

maken made maked maad *make, cause,* 184; *compose, draw up,* 325. See note l. 95.

maladye *ailment, malady*

male *wallet, bag*

man *man,* 167

maner *sort, kind.* See note l. 71

manhod *manhood, manliness*

manly *manly.* See note l. 167

mantel *cloak*

marchal *master of the ceremonies, steward*

marchant *merchant*

mariage *marriage, wedding*

martir *martyr*

marybones *marrow-bones*

matere *matter, business*

maunciple *manciple.* See note l. 567

may *may.* See **mowen**

mayde *maid, girl*

mede *reward*

medlee see note l. 328

meede *meadow*

meeke *modest*

melodye *melody, song*

men *one.* Used to make passive voice. See **man**

mene *mean*

mercenarie *hireling*

mere *mare*

merye mery mury myrie *merry*

meschief *mischief, misfortune*

mesurable *moderate, temperate*

mete *food*, 136; *mealtime*, 127

mewe *coop*

might *power*

mighte see also **mowen**

mighty *strong, powerful*

milk *milk*

millere *miller*

miscarie *come to harm*

mister *craft, trade*

mo *more*

moneye *money*

monk *monk, member of a monastic order*

month *month*

moo *more*

moone *moon*

moore *in greater measure, to a greater degree*

moost *especially, in very large measure*

moot moote mote *must, ought* 232, 742, 832; **moste:** *had to,* 712

moral *moral, godly*

mormal *inflamed sore*

morne *morning*

morsel *portion, fragment*

mortal *deadly*

mortreux See note l. 384

morwe *morning*

moste see **moot**

mote see **moot**

motteley *striped clothing.* See note l. 271

mous *mouse*

mouth *mouth*

mowen may mighte *be able*

moyste *soft, pliable,* 457; *moisture,* 420

muche *great*

muchel *greatly, a great amount, a great deal*

mury see **merye**

murierly *the more merrily*

myn *my, mine*

myre *mire*

myrie see **merye**

myrthe *amusement, merriment, jest*

myselven *myself*

nacion *nation*

namo *no more*

naretten see **aretten**, and note l. 726

narwe *narrow, close together.* See note l. 625

nas see **been**

nat *not*

natheless *nevertheless, none the less*

natureel *natural.* See note l. 416

nature *nature, disposition, kind*

naught *none*

ne *nor*

neden *be necessary*

neede *necessary*

neer *nearer*

neet *cattle*

neighebour *neighbour*

nekke *neck*

never nevere *never*

newe *new, fashionable, modern,* 176; *newly, recently,* 365

nightertale *night-time*

nightyngale *nightingale*

noble *notable, distinguished, noble*

noght *not at all, by no means*

nolde see **shal**

nombre *number*

nones *occasion, time.* See note l. 379

nonne *nun*

noon *none, no one*

noot see **wite**

norissyng *nourishment*

nose *nose*

nosethirles *nostrils*

note *tune, note*

not-heed *closely cropped head*
nowthe *now, at the moment*
now *now*
nowher *nowhere*
ny *closely*
nyce *fastidious, scrupulous*
nyne *nine*
o *one*
obstinat *obstinate*
of *of, about, within,* 87; *some,* 146
offertorie *see note l.* 710
office *secular employment*
offrynge *offering.* See note l. 450
ofte *many*
ofteyme *often*
oghte *ought*
old *old.* See note l. 476
ones *one and the same time*
oon *one, the same.* See note l. 341
ooth *oath*
open *open*
opinioun *opinion*
ordre *monastic order, order of friars*
other *other*
othes *see* **ooth**
ounce *small piece, bunch*
oure *our*
out *out, far and wide*
outrely *entirely, utterly, without gainsaying*
outrydere *rider out.* See note l. 166
overest *upper, uppermost, topmost*
overal *everywhere, wherever*
overlippe *top lip, upper lip*
oversprede overspradde *spread over*
owen *owe, own*
owher *anywhere*
owne *own*
oynement *ointment*
oynon *onion*
oystre *oyster*
paas *pace, walking pace*
pace *go, pass, outstrip*
pacient *patient*

pale *pale*
palfrey *palfrey, saddle-horse*
palmere *palmer.* See note l. 13
pardee *By God*
pardoner *pardoner.* See note l. 669
pardon *pardon, indulgence*
parfit *perfect*
parisshe *parish*
parisshen *parishioner*
partrich *partridge*
parvys *church porch.* See note l. 310
passen *pass, surpass, cross, outstrip*
patente *patent.* See note l. 315
paye *pay*
pecok *peacock*
pees *peace*
peire *set, string, rosary*
penaunce *penance*
peple *people*
perce *pierce*
perchaunce *indeed, perhaps*
pers *bluish-grey*
person persone persoun *parson, parish priest,* 478; *person,* 521
pestilence *plague time, epidemic*
peynen *take pains, endeavour*
philosophre *philosopher, alchemist.* See note l. 297
philosophye *philosophy*
phisyk *medicine*
pigges *pigs*
piled *deprived of, plucked, scanty*
pilwe-beer *pillow case*
pin *pin*
pinchen *cavil at,* 326; *pleat,* 151
pitaunce *portion of food*
pitous *compassionate, full of pity*
plentevous *abundant, plenteous*
plesaunt *pleasing, agreeable*
plesen *please*
pleyen *play, amuse oneself, jest*
pleyn *absolute, full,* 315; *fully,* 327
pleyn *plainly*
pleynly *openly*

plowman *ploughman, small farmer.*
  See note l. 529
point *point,* 114 *condition,* 200
pomely *dappled*
pompe *ostentation, display*
pope *pope, person of authority*
poraille *poor people, rabble*
port *bearing, manner, demeanour*
post *pillar, support*
pouch *pouch, purse*
poudre *powder*
poudre-marchant *flavouring
  powder.* See note l. 381
pouren *pore over, study closely*
povre *poor*
power *power, authority*
poynaunt *pungent, piquant, highly
  flavoured*
poynt *condition*
practisour *practitioner*
prechen *preach*
preest *priest*
prelaat *prelate, ecclesiastic*
press *press, mould, machine*
preyen *pray*
preyere *prayer*
prikasour *hard rider.* But see note
  l. 189
priken *spur, incite*
prikyng *tracking a hare by its
  footprints.* See note l. 189
prioress *prioress, head of a convent.*
  See note l. 118
prively *secretly*
profit *advantage, profit*
propre *own*
proprely *exactly, accurately*
proven *prove true, stand the test of
  experience*
prys *reputation, renown, esteem, price,
  prize*
pullen *pull.* See note ll. 177 and
  652
pultrye *poultry*
punysshe *punish*

purchacen *buy*
purchas *buy*
purchas see note l. 256
purchasour *buyer up of land*
purchasyng *transaction of buying
  up land*
purfile *trim, edge*
purs *money bag, purse*
purtreye *draw, portray*
pye *pie*
quik *lively, animated*
quod *said*
quiksilver *mercury*
quyte *reward, pay, repay*
rage *behave noisily, romp*
rake *rake*
ram *sign Aries in the Zodiac,* 8; *prize
  for wrestling,* 548
rather *by preference, sooner*
raughte see **rechen**
rebel *rebellious*
rechen raughte *reach out*
recchelees *negligent, careless*
recorde *recall, bring to memory*
reden *advise,* 741; *read,* 709
redy *ready, prepared*
reed *adviser, counsellor,* 665; *red,* 90
reherce *rehearse, relate*
rekene *reckon, calculate*
rekenyng *account*
religioun *religion*
relik *relic*
remedyes *potions, charms*
remenaunt *remainder*
rennen ran *run*
rennyng *running*
renoun *reputation*
rente *income.* See note l. 256
repentaunt *repentant, contrite,
  penitent*
reportour *umpire, judge*
reserve *reserve, keep*
reson *opinion, reason, common sense*
reste *rest, bed*

reule *monastic discipline, rule,* 173; *rule, control, guide,* 816

reve *reeve.* See note l. 587

reverence *honour, reverence, respect, respectful manner*

reyn *rain*

reyse *go on a military expedition, see service*

riche *rich,* 311; *rich people,* 248

right *exactly, very*

robes *robe*

roialliche *in a regal manner, as would become a princess*

rood see **ryden**

roos see **rysen**

roost *roast meat*

rooste rosted *to roast*

roote *root*

rote *a small harp,* 236; *rote, heart,* 327

rouncy *a hack, nag, a poor sort of horse*

round *round*

rounded *took a round form.* See note l. 263

route *company*

rudeliche *roughly, rudely broadly*

ruste *grow rusty, deteriorate*

rusty *rusty*

ryde rood riden *ride, rode*

ryse roos *rise, rose*

sake *sake*

sangwyn *blood-red,* 333; *stuff of a blood-red colour,* 439

saugh see **seen**

sautrie *psaltery*

save *except,* 683; *save from penalty,* 661

sawcefleem *pimpled.* See note l. 625

scalled *scabby, scurfy*

scarsly *frugally, sparely*

scathe *harm, misfortune, pity*

science *knowledge*

sclendre *slight*

scole *school*

scoler *student*

scoleye *to attend the university schools, study*

seche *seek*

see *sea*

seege *siege*

seek sike *sick, ill*

seen saugh seigh *see*

seigh see **seen**

seken see **seche**

selle *barter, exchange*

selleres *sellers*

semen *seem*

semely *seemly, suitably, becomingly*

semycope *short cape*

sendal *a fine silk*

senden *send*

sene *visible*

sentence *import, meaning*

sergeaunt *sergeant.* See note l. 309

servant *retainer*

serve *serve, profit*

servysable *anxious to serve*

service servyce *service,* 250; *liturgy,* 122

seson *season*

sessiouns *sessions of the law-courts*

sethe *seethe, boil*

sette *place, arrange, set*

seye seyn seith sayde *say*

seyl *sail*

shadwen *shade*

shal sholde *must, shall, should*

shame *disgrace*

shamefastness *shyness, modesty*

shapen *prepare, intend*

shaply *fit*

sharply *severely*

shave *shave*

sheef *sheaf*

sheeld *a French coin, écu*

shene *bright, beautiful*

sheren *cut, shear*

shinne *shin*

shipman *sailor*

shire *county, shire*

shirreve *sheriff*

shiten *defiled, foul, filthy*

sho *shoe, or perhaps sou, a coin*

shoes *shoes*

sholde see **shal**

shoon see **shynen**

short *short*

shorte *shorten*

shortly *in brief, in a few words*

short-sholdred *thick-set, short-necked*

shour *shower*

shryven *shrive, absolve*

shulder *shoulder*

shynen shoon *shine, shone*

signe *sign, token*

sike see **seek**

sikerly *surely, certainly*

siknesse *sickness, illness*

simple *modest*

singen song songe *sing*

sinne *sin, wicked conduct*

sire *master, sir*

sitten sat sittynge *sit*

sleen slayn *slay, kill*

sleighte *cunning, trickery, craft*

slepen *sleep*

sleves *sleeves*

smal *small, little, fine*

smerte *smartly*

smerten smerte *smart, sting, hurt*

smothe *smooth, 690; smoothly, 676*

smylyng *smiling*

snewen *snow, abound*

snybben *reprove, reprimand, snub*

sobrely *demurely, sedately, soberly*

softe *soft*

solaas *cheer, amusement, pleasure*

solempne *pompous, important, festive. See note l. 209*

solempnely *pompously*

som *some, a certain*

somdel *somewhat, a little*

somer *summer*

somnour *summoner. See note l. 623*

somtyme *formerly, once*

somwhat *a little*

sondry *sundry, different, various*

sone *son*

song *song, anthem*

song see **singen**

sonne *sun*

soo, so *in this manner*

soore *sorely, bitterly*

soote *sweet*

sooth *truth*

soothly *truly, candidly*

sop *sop, soaked bread*

soper *supper*

sort *lot, destiny, fate*

sothe *truly*

soule *soul*

soun *sound*

souynge *talking loudly about, proclaiming. See note l. 275*

souple *supple, soft, pliable*

sovereyn *very high, supreme*

sowe *sow, pig*

sowen sowed *sow*

sownen *sound*

space *opportunity, 35; space of time, 87; course, 176. See note l. 176*

spade *spade*

spak see **speken**

spanne *span, eight inches*

sparen *spare, shirk, refrain from*

sparwe *sparrow*

speche *speech, language, choice of words*

special *special. See note l. 440*

specially *in particular*

speden *prosper, give success*

speken spak *speak*

spenden *spend*

spere *spear*

spiced *scrupulous, hypercritical, sophisticated*

spore *spur*

spryngen *spring, break*
squyer *squire.* See note l. 79
staat *state, condition, estate*
stable *stable, stall*
staf *staff, stick*
stature *stature, height*
statut *statute, law*
stede *place*
stelen *steal*
stemen *shine, gleam*
stepe *bright, glittering, prominent*
sterre *star*
stewe *fishpond*
stif *strong, harsh*
stonden *stand, be placed,* 88; *abide by,* 778
stoon *stone*
stoor *store, stock of cattle*
storie *story*
stot *nag, cob*
stout *stout, strong*
straunge *foreign, strange*
streight *straightway, straight*
streit *strict, narrow*
streite *tightly*
strem *stream,* 464; *current,* 402
strengthe *strength*
strike *hank of flax*
stronde *shore, strand*
studie *study, learning,* 303; *study,* 184. See note l. 841
styward *steward*
substaunce *possessions, personal property*
subtilly *craftily, cunningly*
suffisaunce *sufficiency*
superfluitee *excess, superfluity*
surcote *over-coat, coat worn over another, surcoat*
surgerye *surgery*
swan *swan*
swerd *sword*
swere swore *swear, affirm.* See note l. 810
swete *sweet, fragrant*

swetely *pleasantly*
swich *such*
swift *swift, rapid*
swyn *swine, pigs*
swynk swink *toil, work, labour*
swynken *work, toil*
swynkere *toiler, worker*
syde *side*
syn *since*
sythe *time*
taak see **taken**
tabard *tabard, sleeveless coat worn by a herald,* 20; *smock,* 541
taffata *taffeta, fine silk*
taille *credit, tally.* See note l. 570
taken take taak *take*
takel *tackle, archery gear, bows and arrows*
tale *tale*
talen *tell tales*
tapicer *upholsterer, tapestry maker*
tappestere *barmaid*
targe *small shield*
tart *sharp-tasting, bitter, acid*
tartre *tartar*
taryynge *delay*
taughte see **techen**
tavernes *taverns*
techen taughte taught *teach*
techyng *teaching*
tellen *tell, relate*
tempest *storm*
temple *inn of court, temple*
tendre *tender, pitiful, piteous*
terme *legal phraseology, precise terms*
text *authority, quotation, saying*
teyen *tie; teyd tied*
than thanne *then, than*
thank *thank you, acknowledgment*
tharray see **array**
thencrees see **encrees**
ther *there*
theras *where*
therfore *for that purpose, therefore*
therof *concerning that matter*

theron *thereupon*
therto *moreover*
therupon *thereupon*
therwith *by means thereof*
therwithal *by means thereof*
thikke *thick-set*
thilke *this same*, 182. See **ilke**
thing *legal document*, 325; *thing, obstacle*, 276
thinken *think of*
thinken *seem, appear*; **thinketh**: *it seems*; **thoughte**: *it seemed*
thinne *thin*
tho *those*
thoght *thought*
thombe *thumb*. See note l. 563
thonder *thunder*
though *although*, 68; *if*, 553
thoughte see **thinken**
thresshen *thresh*
thryes *three times*
thriftily *carefully*
til *to*
tipet *short cape, tippet*
togidre *together*
tollen *take payment, take toll*
to-morwe *to-morrow*
tonge *tongue*
tope *top, head*
toun *town, district, village*
trappe *snare, trap*
tretys *long, well-shaped*
trewe *true, honest, faithful*
trewely *faithfully, honestly*, 481; *certainly, indeed*, 761
trompe *trumpet*
trouthe *truth, loyalty*
trowen *believe, should say*
trussen *pack*
tukken *tuck up*. See note l. 621
twelf *twelve*
tweye *twain, two*
twinne *depart*
tyde *tide*
tyme *time*

tythes *tithes, a tax of one-tenth of the produce of the land*
undergrowe *undersized, short of stature*
understonden *understand*
undertake *affirm, am sure, dare say, vow, undertake*
unknowe *unknown*
untrewe *incorrectly, untruly, untruthfully*
usage *practice, use, custom*
vavasour *sub-vassal, vassal of a vassal*
venerye *hunting*
verdit *verdict, decision*
vernicle *vernicle*. See note l. 685
verraily *truly, indeed*
verray *true*. See note l. 72
vertu *power to produce, vitalizing power*
vertuous *capable, respectable, well-to-do*
veyl *veil*
veyne *vein of a plant*
viage *journey, expedition, voyage*
vigilies *vigils, meetings on the eve of a festival*
vileynye *any conduct unbecoming a knight, unseemly behaviour, lack of breeding, ungentlemanly speech*
visage *face*
vitaille *victuals, provisions*
vouche-sauf *grant, permit*
voys *voice*
waiten *look, set store by, require, be cautious*
walet *wallet*
wan see **winnen**
wandrynge *travelling*. See note l. 467
wantown *gay, uncontrolled, carefree*
wantownesse *freak, affectation*
war *aware, prudent, wary*
wastel breed *choice bread*. See note l. 147

waterlees *without water, out of water*
wateryng *place where horses were watered*
webbe *weaver*
weep see **wepen**
weel see **wel**
wel *well*, 29; *some*, 24
welcome *welcome*
wenden wente *go, journey*
wepen weep *weep*
wepynge *weeping*
were weren see **been**
were *wear*
werk *work*
werken wroght wroghte *work, act*
werre *war*. See note l. 47
werte *wart*
west *west country*
wetten *wet*
wex *wax*
wey *way, route, journey, road*
weyen weyede *weigh*
whan *when*
what *what? what sort of a?*, 40; *why?*, 184
whelke *pimple, spot*
whelpe *puppy, cub*
wher-with *whereby, means with which*
which *which? whom? of what sort?*
whil *while*
whilom *formerly, once*
whistlynge *whistling*
whyte *white*
widwe *widow*
wight *person, man*
willen wol wolde *will, desire, intend*
winnen wan wonne *win, gain*
winning *winnings, gain, profit*
wisdom *wisdom, knowledge, learning*
wit *intelligence*
witen woot wiste *know*

withalle *withal, moreover*
withholden *retain*
withouten *without, not counting, excluding*
withseyen *gainsay, contradict, oppose*
wo *sorrow, trouble, woe*
wol see **willen**
wolden see **willen**
womman *women*
wonder *wondrous, wonderfully*, 483; *wonder, marvel*, 402
wonderly *wonderfully, unusually, remarkably*
wone *wont, custom, habit*
wonen wonynge *dwell*
wonyng *dwelling, house*
wood *mad*
woodecraft *forestry, hunting*
worldly *worldly*. See note l. 292
worstede *worsted, a kind of wool*
worth *worth*, 182; *worth while*, 785
worthy *distinguished, respectable, well-to-do*
worthinesse *distinction, prowess*
wrastlynge *wrestling match*
wrighte *workman*
writ *what is written, the Scriptures*
writen *write*
wroght see **werken**
wrooth *angry*
wyd *wide, scattered, spacious*
wyf *woman, wife*
wympel *wimple, a covering for the neck*. See note l. 151
wyn *wine*
wynnen see **winnen**
wypen wyped *wipe*
wys *discreet, prudent, wise*
y- a prefix often used for the past participle
yaf see **yeve**
y-bore see **bere**
y-cleped see **clepen**
y-come see **comen**

ye *eye*

ye yow *you*

yeddynges *songs, ballads.* See note
l. 237

yeer *year, years*

yeldhalle *guildhall, hall belonging to
a guild*

yeldynge *yield, produce*

yelow *yellow*

yeman *yeoman.* See note l. 101

yemanly *in yeomanlike fashion, as a
yeoman should*

yerde *yardstick, rod*

yet *yet, nevertheless*

yeven yaf *give*

y-falle see **fallen**

y-go see **goon**

y-knowe see **knowen**

y-lad see **leden**

y-lyk *like*

ymage *image.* See note l. 411

ynogh *enough*

yong *young*

yow see **ye**

y-punysshed see **punysshe**

y-preved see **proven**

y-purfiled see **purfile**

y-ronne see **rennen**

y-sene see **sene**

y-shadwed see **shadwen**

y-shave see **shave**

y-shorn see **sheren**

y-shrive see **shryven**

y-taught see **techen**

y-teyd see **teyen**

y-wroght see **werken**

y-wympled see **wympel**